To Betty, Dick +

This is your last chance.

Le

The Family Therapy Collections

James C. Hansen, Series Editor

Lee Combrinck-Graham, MD, Volume Editor

TREATING YOUNG CHILDREN IN FAMILY THERAPY

AN ASPEN PUBLICATION®
Aspen Publishers, Inc.
Rockville, Maryland
Royal Tunbridge Wells
1986

Library of Congress Cataloging in Publication Data
Main entry under title:

Treating young children in family therapy.

(The Family therapy collections: 18)
"An Aspen publication."
Bibliography: p. Includes index.

1. Family psychotherapy. 2. Child psychotherapy.
I. Combrinck-Graham, Lee. II. Series.
RC488.5.T72   1986   618.92′89′156   86-10724
ISBN: 0-89443-618-X

The Family Therapy Collections series is indexed in
Psychological Abstracts and the PsycINFO database

Library of Congress Catalog Card Number: 86-10724
Editorial Services: Ruth Bloom
ISBN: 0-89443-618-X
ISSN: 0735-9152

Printed in the United States of America

1 2 3 4 5

Table of Contents

Board of Editors

v

Series Preface

THE FAMILY THERAPY COL-LECTIONS is a quarterly publication in which topics of current and specific interest to family therapists are presented. Each volume contains articles authored by practicing professionals, providing in-depth coverage of a single aspect of family therapy. This volume focuses on involving children in family therapy.

Although one would assume that all family members participate in family therapy, a younger child is often excluded—even when that child is the symptomatic person. Whether or not the child is symptomatic, considerable information about family dynamics is hidden if the child is not present. The presence of all the children in the family helps the therapist to understand the role of each child in the family system. Adults often fail to see life through the eyes of a child, and that perspective sometimes makes a difference in family therapy. Involving children in family therapy is more effective when the therapist is comfortable in working with children, however, and can place a child's behavior in context.

This volume provides not only information about the inclusion of young children in family therapy, but also information about several children's problems and illustrations of methods of family therapy in which young children are included. It contains a wealth of practical case studies and examples that the reader can generalize to other types of problems.

Lee Combrinck-Graham, M.D., is the volume editor. Dr. Combrinck-Graham received her training in child psychiatry at the Philadelphia Child Guidance Clinic. She has been employed at the Philadelphia Child Guidance Clinic, has worked in private practice, and is presently the director of the Master of Family Therapy program of Hahnemann University. Dr. Combrinck-Graham has selected outstanding therapists and authors to develop a volume rich in information for therapists who treat children in family therapy.

James C. Hansen
Series Editor

Preface

IT HAS ALWAYS BEEN MY BE-lief that children make a family; yet family therapy is often practiced without children present. There are many reasons that this very important population has so frequently been excluded from family therapy. Sources of the problems seem to be in the historical development of child therapy and family therapy.

Child therapy, derived from adult psychoanalysis, has focused largely on the internal life of the child. The decoding of material presented either through verbalization or through play leads to conclusions about the child's inner state. The therapy is then shaped by the use of symbolic experiences in play and by the relationship between the therapist and the child. One of the problems with this approach is that the therapist does not work with what is manifest in the system, but with what is theoretical. Furthermore, the therapist replaces the parents in a corrective relationship with the child, placing the burden of responsibility for the problem within the child and then depriving the child of his or her most crucial resources—the parents.

Recently, child therapy has expanded to include the important mother-child interaction. The relatively new field of infant psychiatry is really mother-of-infant psychiatry in that the infant's emotional development is believed to result from the mother's management of the attachment, bonding, emerging separation, and individuation processes. Thus, many modern child therapists report that they are seeing "families," when they are actually seeing the mother, often without the child. Mothers do not make a family, however, and surely they are not solely responsible for what their children are.

Two problems have emanated from the strange association of marital with family therapy. One is that marital therapy, which deals with dyads, is often mistakenly called family therapy, which deals with triads. The other is that, because marital therapists deal with adult couples, they conveniently understand family dysfunction as marital dysfunction and work accordingly. Most would agree that young children have no place in marital therapy. Thus, while the child therapist implicitly places the problem inside the child, the marital therapist assumes that child dysfunction results from a problem in the marriage. In this case, parents bear the entire burden of their children's difficulties.

Another problem for many family therapists is that they have little training in working with children; therefore, they tend to avoid it, if possible. Besides a background in child development, working with children requires such skills as common sense, an ability to play, and a tolerance for fun.

In order to bridge some of these chasms, this volume of the Family Therapy Collections is devoted to the subject of young children in family therapy. It gives the clinician many case studies, addressing many very troublesome problems of childhood.

Edited works begin with careful planning and develop *pari passu*, and this volume is no exception. The collection is rather like a pot luck supper. Everyone has brought a dish, and the result is a richly varied, but balanced feast in which there are bound to be things for everyone's taste.

Keith tantalizes the reader who wants to know why the children should participate in family therapy and what to do when they get there. Keith says that the therapist can do without the children, of course, but once there, they have a great deal to contribute.

For the reader who is interested in the more radical systems approach to treatment, Giacomo and Weissmark describe childhood itself as a context with its attendant paradoxes, and Combrinck-Graham's commitment to treating what can be seen between people rather than what is imagined within them is of interest.

For the reader who believes that family therapy is fine for the simple behavior problems of childhood, but more heavy-duty therapies are necessary for the more serious and chronic disorders, Lindblad-Goldberg, Bartholemew, Lewis, Foster, Seelig, and Brendler present examples of the most difficult and disturbed childhood contexts, demonstrating approaches to strengthen the family system while addressing other systems involved with the child and family.

For the reader who is concerned that the individual needs of the child are neglected in family therapy, Foster demonstrates her skill at developmental assessment in a family context and calls for attention to the children in family therapy. Keith, Combrinck-Graham, and Brendler "listen" to the behavioral commentary of the child, and Seelig discusses the combination of residential and educational contexts in family therapy, specifically addressing the children's perceptions of themselves.

This collection illustrates what I have long believed: Family systems therapy directed, as it is, at children's most significant human resources is the best hope for dealing with the most difficult problems of childhood and, thus, offers much for the future. Our children are the future, but they are also the present. Children develop fast; they cannot wait for us to make the world a better place for them in the future. It is necessary to include the children in family therapy to make their world a better place in the present.

I would like to thank the contributors to this volume. Their cooperation, their cheerfulness about deadlines and revisions, and their enthusiasm for the enterprise of this volume have made the entire process smooth and satisfying.

Lee Combrinck-Graham, MD
June 1986

1

Are Children Necessary in Family Therapy?

David V. Keith, MD
Family Therapy Institute, Inc.
St. Paul, Minnesota

C HILDREN HAVE A POWER-ful, though implicit, effect on culture as the following story, told by Lewis Thomas (1983), illustrates.

Late in the nineteenth century, thousands of immigrant workers were brought to Hawaii from all over Asia and the South Pacific to work in the sugar industry. A community crisis developed out of the inability to communicate because of the diversity of languages represented. A "pidgin" language emerged; a language of nouns. Things could be named, but there was no grammatical structure for conveying ideas. Mysteriously, within a single generation a complex new language emerged called Hawaiian Creole. Linguists believe this language developed from the children's playing together. While the adults sat around campfires talking in the limited pidgin language, the children danced in the background shouting and playing, and making up rhymes. Out of this spontaneous process came a new language.

The special contribution of children to the process of family therapy is often overlooked. It is useful to retrace the professional path which led to the ideas I am presenting here.

My medical career began as an Air Force flight surgeon—the pilots' doctor. My job was to "keep 'em flying" and medical care methods were predicated on maintaining health as opposed to caring for the ill. The interconnections between mind, body and social structure were unavoidable considerations. The Air Force oriented me to thinking systemically, but without a theoretical framework.

1

When I entered psychiatry residency, after the Air Force, I had two contradictory experiences. While on the one hand, I was discovering how to utilize family therapy in psychiatry, on the other, I took a silent oath that I would never become a child psychiatrist. From our conference room we were deciding the fate of another troubled child, hoping for the best but fearing the worst. Recommendations were usually predicated on what the community was going to do for the child, while the child and most of the people responsible for that child's fate were not present. In my family therapy work, I particularly enjoyed the fun of having children in therapy sessions, whether on the inpatient psychiatry unit to help with father's depression, on the medical ward in relation to mother's poorly controlled high blood pressure, or in the pediatric clinic about the son's stealing. With children in the interviews, psychiatry lost its cross-sectional quality and an elusive, developmental perspective emerged. It was easier to get past impasses imposed by worrying about a pain with a hidden cause or who was to blame. Impasses that developed in these cases were related equally to the chains on our intellect and the dynamics of the family. The children often brought magic that helped us to escape, Houdini-like, from these impasses. Besides, when the children were there the interviews were livelier.

I was fascinated by the mutual effect of children and family systems which was family therapy. Child psychiatry, in contrast, felt discouraging. For me, the difference between family therapy and child psychiatry was like the difference between being an aeronautical engineer and being a pilot. I was more interested in flying than design. Since family therapy seemed outside the psychiatric mainstream, I broke my secret oath about child psychiatry, in hopes of gaining more credibility in the framework of the medical context in which I work.

I entered child psychiatry to augment my work as a family therapist. I was a family therapist before I became a child psychiatrist. I do not worry about the children as individuals as I do about keeping the family flying—the pattern learned from my Air Force experience. If the family collapses and loses its capacity for parenting, the children's development is likely to be impaired. Meeting the needs of the children in the family is not a project separate from working with the family as a whole, because I know that if the health of the family expands so does the children's health. Children need to be included in any family therapy project not because it benefits the children, but because their inclusion enhances the family's potential for change.

Family therapists who are not trained in children's health are naturally shy about including children in the family therapy sessions. They forget that children are just people—only more so. The spontaneity that children add may cause confusion so that the therapist feels incompetent. But confusion is the doorway to change: it allows other faces of the self to emerge. In this sense, including the children in sessions really changes the mission of the therapy away from what is often labored assessment and movement towards carefully developed goals. If I had become a child psychiatrist before I became a flight surgeon, I might see therapy this way myself. Instead I see it much more like plowing a field, turning over the soil, sowing the seed, and letting nature take its course.

Winnicott (1971, p. 38) said that psychotherapy is two people playing together. If the family does not know how to play, the aim of therapy is to teach them. The opposite of play is to be purposeful. Every parent knows that it is impossible to parent purposefully. The process of parenting involves frequent episodes of "going out of your head." When children enter family therapy, they are apt to disrupt the therapist's conscious purpose. Including the children adds confusion—the beginning of playing together.

AN EXERCISE IN PSYCHIATRIC SOPHISTRY

What are children? Being attached to a family is part of the definition of a child. They are sweet, innocent, and demanding. They teach us how to love and expose us to our rage. They steal time, order, logic, and self-esteem. They expand self-esteem, enhance the family, and press for its destruction. They bring their parents closer together, and they drive their parents apart. They change the patterns of language in the family. Their impact is symbolic in a way that embraces contradiction.

The mythical story of the birth of Hermes (a.k.a. Mercury) creates a useful image of children (Stein, 1983). This mixed-up image partially illuminates the ambivalent response we have to children. Hermes was one of Zeus' sons, Apollo's little brother. Shortly after his birth, Hermes went for a walk by the sea, alone. He came upon a turtle, killed it, and made a lyre out of the shell, thereby inventing music. (Impressive for a child who has not been to Montessori!) Then he found the herd of prize cattle that belonged to his big brother, Apollo. He took 50 away and hid them. His ten o'clock feeding was approaching, so he killed two of the cattle to eat. Then the little baby returned to his mother and the cave where he was born and fell asleep in his cradle. Apollo, very upset by the loss of his cattle, learned that Hermes had stolen them. Apollo went to the cave and accused the infant. Hermes replied, "But I am just a baby, how could I steal your cattle? Even if I knew what a cattle was?" The weak little innocent turned the world on its ear. But how? In such power lies the seductive mystery of children.

Children are intuitive guides to the shared unconscious of the family. When children are included in family therapy, boundaries of time, person, generation, and meaning become fluid. The parents, seeing themselves as children, slide back into associations from their childhood. As the image of potential transformation, the child prepares the way for future change in the personality of the family and its members, anticipating the integration of conscious and unconscious elements. The child is the symbol that unites opposites, such as the family of the mother and the family of the father, male and female, past and future. The child is the mediator, the healer, the one who makes the picture whole. Disruption and fragmentation may precede renewed integration, however, as psychic birth follows no obvious pathway (Jung & Kerenyi, 1973).

The child's "Alice in Wonderland" world is distorted, but accurate. Children are automatically at the symbolic level in the metaphorical world of multiple meanings. They force a new honesty on those who want access to their world.

A family with six children, four from the father's first marriage and two from the mother's, sought therapy because the 11-year-old, John, was in trouble at school and in a standoff with everyone in this newly blended family. The interview stalled after 15 minutes. The children were angry about being there. Much to everyone's surprise, John began to weep when the topic of his missing mother was mentioned. The 3-year-old and the 4-year-old began to act out the family's unspoken emotional restlessness. Just then, the 6-year-old daughter discovered the toy cabinet, and the interview process shifted to a different plane as the children immersed themselves in play.

A free-flowing give-and-take developed in the family. The father helped the 5-year-old with a drawing. The mother and two of the other children built a huge block tower. John worked on a piece of clay. The opportunity to play diffused the family's overcautious concern about John, allowing a freer discussion of the family's living patterns, their sadness, and fears. The 6-year-old's fantasy car crash reminded the father of his own frustrated, explosive feelings. One child told her dream about throwing the food in the furnace. The mother was reminded of her own dream in which her mother married her ex-husband. Then the father had a pillow fight with John. At the end of the interview, as all filed out, the parents came last. The mother shook the therapist's hand and said simply, "Thanks for the toys."

INCLUDING CHILDREN: SOME REASONS

- We miss too much of the family process without the children, especially the way that contradictory feelings are blended in family living. Children express needs and feelings in a symbolic, therefore, wholistic way. The family problems are condensed and less differentiated, thus more available for change. We want whole persons at the interview. A reasonable person is not a whole person.

Two divorced parents were having an endless quarrel about who was the best parent and, covertly, who was to blame for the divorce. The 7-year-old said to the therapist, "He thinks she is to blame and she thinks he is to blame. Well I think they are both to blame and they both ought to get a good spanking."

Joan's family sought treatment for her because she was obese and had no friends. The parents' description of Joan and the family seemed very normal, if the therapists could dream she was 10 and not twenty-one. In the middle of the second interview the therapists woke up when Joan gave them a picture she had drawn of a large bug in the middle of a landscape. At the center of the bug was a small door, 1 inch by 2 inches. The door flipped up to reveal a very small replica of the big bug, the little girl hidden inside the pseudo big girl.

- Children are affect barometers. They are not confused by facts, but are oriented to nonverbal signals. They can smell tension, separation, hostility and anxiety. With their over-developed instincts for social adaptation, adults constantly diminish the nonverbal.

After 8 months of therapy, when the divorce was all but final, the attorney who had decided to adopt a homosexual life style after 3 years of marriage was asked by his wife if he could explain the change in his sexual orientation. She asked the question calmly, there was no discernible evidence of anxiety in either parent. A split-second after the wife asked the question the 3-year-old said, "Mommy, let's get out of this house." He had picked up the premonitory signs of anxiety.

A therapist worked with a 4-year-old autistic boy and his parents for nearly a year. The boy was making loud kissing noises as he played in the corner behind the sofa. The therapist was suddenly aware of his strong feelings of affection for the mother at that moment. The child was able to sneak in behind the therapist's professional face.

• The children reduce purposefulness of family therapy and increase access to the unconscious, giving adults the nonrational freedom that leads to deeper integration. Regardless of the presenting complaint in a family with young children, it is not unusual that one of the early interviews ends up with us on the floor playing and talking with one of the children. The family often goes away feeling immensely helped by such a session. We do not understand the process; it makes little

sense, except to think that there is an extended right-brain process in effect. It is akin to the way the parents move when the therapist cuddles their baby. The parents are apt to stretch comfortably as if they were being cuddled.

The Does had completed 8 months of effective couple therapy. The marriage had been enlivened, and both had delved deeply and richly into their background families. They were now concerned about Joe, their 9-year-old son, whose tantrums and demands were intruding on their marriage. Their new togetherness no longer required his omnipotent domination. The marital therapist referred them to family therapy and formed a cotherapy team with the family therapist. Mrs. Doe was a very bright, hypercompetent advertising executive. Mr. Doe was a tall Anthony Perkins type, soft, and very careful with Mrs. Doe. Couple therapy had moved him into the middle of the marriage, however tentatively. Two interviews went well as the therapists both attended to and ignored Joe and his more subdued sister. At the end of the first session, Joe, who had resisted coming and participated only grudgingly, now refused to leave, thereby "one-upping" his parents again. When they returned for the second interview, Mrs. Doe wanted to get down to business, but the therapist stayed indirectly relevant and in a play mode. "I need goals, I need direction. Where are we going?" she complained. "The purpose is to learn how to be purposeless," the therapist replied, with a straight face. "I've never heard of anything like that," she says. "Welcome to a new idea," answered the therapist. "I meant, apart from a cocktail party," Mrs. Doe ended. Two days before the third interview, the Does made a call to their marital therapist. "We want goals," was the repeated complaint. Mrs. Doe found a psychology graduate student to help develop a behavior modification program for Joe. The therapists felt as if they were dealing with her omnipotence, the precursor of the son's behavior. She was suspicious of complexity and restless with the therapists' kind of ambiguity. She was confused and did not like it, but her confusion was evidence of a metashift. When the family appeared for the third interview, Mr. Doe was changed in several ways. He had started a beard, and was expansive about it. He also talked about how much he had enjoyed his son during the preceding week. The detoxified demon played on the floor between the cotherapists. That was the last interview, and a phone call from Mrs. Doe six weeks later suggested things had gone well at home, even with the behavior modification program.

- The presence of children in family therapy defines the family as an integrated whole with a generation gap. When the 18-year-old son comes home from college and joins the therapy session, for example, the coalitions are likely to shift. The father, who has seemed so isolated, suddenly has a partner. The same change occurs when the children are added to a couple. Ages are unimportant.

- There is a palpable *we* when two generations are present. It is probably the family's job to protect its members from the community and to help them to fit into the community, even though these motives are contradictory. One of the risks of individual therapy is that it may inadvertently disrupt the "We," either by removing the scapegoat from the family, or by combining with a family member in a manner emphasizing the inadequacies of the other family members. There is no substitute for the family, however. One of the important contributions of family therapy is to define a "We" with the power and authority to care for itself and its members.

- The children's worry about the parents is equal to the parents' worry about the children, although the children's concern is usually hidden and expressed covertly. Likewise, the parents' distrust of the children is equal to the children's distrust of the parents. Again, the children's distrust is expressed covertly.

The Hamptons' 11-year-old son was arrested for shop-lifting; 2 weeks later, he was arrested for vandalizing 2 cars in the neighborhood. The family sought therapy. It was not until the third interview that Mr. Hampton's heart attack of the preceding year was revealed. He had not allowed the family to talk about it at home or in the office. When the topic was raised, every family member, except Mr. Hampton, talked with animation and emotion. Mrs. Hampton was frightened that the next heart attack was just around the corner. The 11-year-old was in tears, fearing his father's death. It was a relief to have the issue out in the open. Still, Mr. Hampton was upset with the family for talking about his coronary and with the therapist for linking it to his son's behavior. He appeared at the next interview without his family and tried to dissuade the therapist from any further discussion.

This is a dramatic example of a frequent occurrence. The parents reluctantly bring the child in for treatment only to learn that the child is worried about their divorce, the father's coronary, or the mother's depression. It is inevitable to wonder whether children are injured by exposure to the parents' stresses. The children's fantasies and nightmares are much worse than reality (C.A. Whitaker, 1973).

• Communication of difficult questions or information is enhanced by the presence of the children. This is particularly true when a family member is facing death.

The marriage was cold and the parents distant nonpersons. The 8-year-old child, Joe, was overcharged with affect, hyperactive, and the subject of the parents' constant concern. The therapist talked with the child about his parents. "Do you think your mother is prettier with her glasses on or off? Has your father always been crazy like this? He never giggles." This silly, mundane talk relaxed the boy who moved over by the therapist and began a drawing. With Joe out of the middle, the wife's anger at the

husband's depressive unavailability erupted. The father retaliated by accusing the mother of an epic-making turn-off 3 years earlier. The boy continued drawing. He did not even need to be hyperactive.

• Children open up and humanize the vulgarity and sadistic backlands in the family.

The squeaky clean, moralistic family was proceeding carefully through the third interview. The junior high daughters were tormenting the 6-year-old son with "grundies" (i.e., grabbing his underwear waist band and pulling forcefully upward). The parents grew more and more agitated when the torture did not stop. In frustration the mother coached the son, "Pinch their nipples! Pinch their nipples!" While there was no further discussion about the skirmish afterward, the family (and therapist) had a new ease in exposing the nonpublic components of their lives.

• The presence of the children naturalizes and depathologizes the family context. Individuals are the most of who they are in their families.

The suave, newly uncloseted homosexual attorney and his wife came to the therapist's office. For the first interview the wife appeared frankly paranoid. When their 2-year-old came to the second interview, the wife was much healthier and the paranoid component that had dominated the first interview was rarely seen, while Mr. Suave turned into Mr. Superficial.

The Hills, both therapists, came with their 3-year-old and 6-year-old boys for a 2-hour consultation about their marriage. The children were unruly and the parents hopelessly over-professionalized. The therapy team waited for enough anxiety to accumulate so the Hills could get clearer about what they wanted. Near the end of the first hour of the parents' useless intellectualizing and impotent, professional child care maneuvering, the older boy threw the younger against the bookshelf, where he hit his head hard and began to shriek. The mother finally reached the end of her patience and began to sob with despair, "This is it. This is what I cannot stand. I just don't know what to do with them when they are like this." Then the father's tears came, followed by his honest concern about his wife, his marriage, and his sons.

While it may be obvious from these case histories that the presence of children aids the therapeutic process for the family, the way that children enhance the experience of the therapist is not so clear. On the other hand, children may cause the therapist to feel and be inept or clumsy. It must be reemphasized that ineptitude may be a symptom of a deeper play experience. It is better to live it through with the family, than to back away from it. Thus, it seems the only reason children should be excluded from family therapy is when their presence adds too much to the therapist's stress.

INCLUDING CHILDREN: SOME PRACTICAL SUGGESTIONS

- It is helpful for the family therapist, especially the new family therapist, to have a cotherapist, when children are included in therapy sessions. The therapist must move slowly with the children, waiting for a clue from them that they are ready for contact. The therapist should signal availability, but avoid being intrusive. Even eye contact can be intrusive if too persistent. A few toys are a valuable medium for communication. Kleenex make an endless series of toys, including hats, missiles, and peek-a-boo masks.

- Respond to children in simple language. If an explanation exceeds two sentences it is too long. One of the quickest ways to alienate children is to ask questions. Questions are depersonalizing. It is best for the therapist just to describe what the kids are doing. It is even better to be slightly inaccurate, so that the children can have the fun of correcting the therapist.

- Children are disruptive in the office when the tension is high in the family and when they sense that the therapist is apprehensive about them. The therapist must respond to disruption at the children's level, even when it is necessary to interrupt work with the parents to work with the children. At such times, the cotherapist is particularly helpful. When younger children are included, it is not unusual for the early interviews to focus mainly on play with them. One of the best ways to deal with younger children is to get down on the floor with them.

- If necessary the history should be interrupted to work with the child. The history can and will wait. It will not change much. On the other hand, the therapist should not let the parents interfere with the work with the children. The parents can be told they do not need to be jealous, their child will be returned at the end of the hour. When the parents coach their child, "Go ahead, you can tell the truth, be honest," they may mean "watch your step." Children know just how honest to be from listening to their parents.

- There is always the question of who should manage the children in the office. It seems best for the therapist to do the parenting during the therapy session. When the therapist manages the children in the office, it gives the parents another model for parenting. There is therapeutic benefit for the parents in seeing their children from a distance. Unconscious distortions imposed by the family dynamics may be washed away. Additionally, the parents do not know the rules in the therapist's office. They are different from the rules at home.

- The therapist should make contact with the children directly, not through the parents. The obvious way is by playing, but contact can also be made by teasing, cajoling, or by laying down the law (and enforcing it). One of the best ways to establish a relationship with children, particularly with adolescents, is to scold them with honesty.

The family was deep in a divorce struggle. The 10-year-old son and 8-year-old daughter were very protective of their mother. When anyone spoke to her, they would distract her or talk to her themselves. The therapist said to the 8-year-old girl, "I am talking to your

mother, and you be quiet when I am talking. You are just a little girl and you have to mind your manners when you are in my office."

- Finally, the therapist should protect the children, but without making them scared. Protection should focus on validating their personhood and liberating them from family projections.

CONCLUSION

The following story is a clinical example of the powerful and covert effect of children on the family culture. It illustrates the invisible effect of children on the family change process.

The Jones, a family of four, entered therapy because they said vaguely, "a lot had been happening" with their family and they wanted a chance to talk. The first interview was unfocused and it was not until the second session that the parents revealed their concern about their 9-year-old daughter, Wendy. They thought Wendy was isolated, moody, and made too many demands. There were additional problems related to the marriage and the in-laws. At the end of the third interview, Wendy complained that she did not want to return for the next interview. "Why should I come? All you do is pick on me." The therapist suggested playfully that she could write a story about the advantages of growing up in a crazy family. Two weeks later the mother called and said that Wendy had finished the story and offered to mail it to the therapist. She mailed in a charming story, awkwardly typed on three single-spaced pages. The story was about a family of four where everyone was unhappy and disagreeable, so they had to go see a psychiatrist. He was no help. When they returned home they found out that the mother was pregnant and she was afraid to tell the daughters. So they went back to the psychiatrist and everything worked out happily. At the bottom of the last page was a handwritten message. "This is not about my family." That was true, in a way, yet the story was symbolically accurate, like a dream. With her story, Wendy captured some concealed essence of the family's worries.

No dramatic change resulted from the story, but there was a transformation in the family's tone. They shifted gears and began preparation, both sad and zestful, for the empty nest. She was the youngest child, and they may have been secretly mourning the loss of their baby to adolescence. In a later session, the parents had a powerful fight which deepened the intimacy between them. The father brought his own widowed father to a subsequent interview. Wendy's story was like a little golden key that opened a box of experiences for the family and their inhibited growing began again.

Are children necessary in family therapy? No. If they have not been around, they will not be missed. But a family is not a family when the children are excluded. The parents are then just a subgroup. Change happens more slowly and is less likely to endure when the family therapist works with a subgroup.

Children find and open the doors to a wonderland hidden directly in the midst of the family. With laughter or tears or great seriousness they slip through the doorway, and if the luck is right, trip the lever so that a trap door opens and the whole family drops in.

BIBLIOGRAPHY

Jung, C.G., & Kerenyi, C. (1973). *Essays on a science of mythology: The myth of the divine child and the mysteries of Eleusis*. Princeton, NJ: Princeton University Press.

Stein, M. (1983). *In midlife: A Jungian perspective*. Dallas, TX: Spring Publications.

Thomas, L. (1983). *Late night thoughts on listening to Mahler's ninth symphony*. New York: Viking Press.

Whitaker, C.A. (1973). Personal communication. Madison, Wisconsin.

Winnicott, D.W. (1971). *Playing and reality*. New York: Basic Books.

2

Coming and Going of Age: Treating Children with Families

Daniel Giacomo, MD
Child and Family Psychiatrist
University of Pennsylvania
Philadelphia, Pennsylvania

Mona Weissmark, PhD
Psychologist
Department of Social Systems Sciences
University of Pennsylvania
and
Clinical Assistant Professor
Hahnemann University
Philadelphia, Pennsylvania

"Who are you?" said the Caterpillar. Alice replied, rather shyly, "I-I hardly know, sir, just at present—at least I know who I was when I got up this morning, but I think I must have been changed several times since then." "What do you mean by that?" said the Caterpillar sternly. "Explain yourself!". "I can't explain myself because I'm not myself, you see." "I don't see," said the Caterpillar. "I'm afraid I can't put it more clearly," Alice replied very politely, "for I can't understand it myself to begin with; and being so many different sizes in a day is very confusing."

Lewis Carroll
Alice's Adventures in Wonderland

C HILDHOOD IS A SOCIAL CONstruct that has evolved through the last three centuries. Implicit in the construct of childhood is a learning context that frames the actions of society's newborns.

From a systemic point of view, a small child can be conceptualized as an evolving system that can generate a great deal of variety* (i.e., number of possible states). Society regulates the potential formation of variety by means of a societal code (e.g., rules, laws, customs). The laws and rules are expressed in absolute statements, such as "Thou shalt not kill." and "Obey thy father and mother." The central mechanisms in the regulation of variety are variety attenuators. These mechanisms function primarily by decreasing and unifying variety. In this attempt to attenuate variety, however, contradictions and inconsistencies may emerge. For example, if one is told to commit a murder by one's father and does so, at least one of the

---

*Variety is the number of possible states of a system. If there are n people in a system, and each of them has variety x, then the variety of the total system thus defined will be x^n. So if there are only 40 people ($n = 40$), each of whom has only two possible states ($x = 2$), there are $2^{40} = 1,099,511,627,776$ possible states.

moral rules "Thou shalt not kill." and "Obey thy father and mother." is semi-absolute. Therefore, there have to be rules that integrate "absolute" statements in situations in which they contradict one another.

THE CONTEXT

Aries (1962) commented that, in the 10th century, artists were unable to depict a child except as a man on a smaller scale. Between that time and the beginning of the 19th century, however, Western society discovered childhood. There was a major transformation in thought and feeling as the child was gradually distinguished from the adult, given a distinctive dress, assigned "childish" games, and protected from open reference to sexual matters.

It was not until the 17th century that the concept of child took on its present meaning. Religious reformers attempted to moralize society by popularizing the idea that, because children were incompetent and innocent, they needed to be protected from promiscuous behavior. Not until then did childhood become anything more than an incidental phase in the developmental pattern. The changing attitude first affected the sons of aristocratic families, but it gradually spread to include the daughters as well and finally transformed the lives of children in all social classes.

The emerging idea of childhood occasioned a massive reorientation of the family and school to focus on children, delayed entrance into adult life, and created a modern world concerned with the physical, moral, and sexual problems of children. The solicitude of the family, church, and school deprived children of the freedom that they had hitherto enjoyed among adults; it inflicted on them the birch and the prison cells—in a word, the punishments usually reserved for convicts. This severity was the expression of an obsessive love that was to dominate society after the 18th century. The growing awareness that children were sui generis laid the basis for a new kind of family.

Aries (1962) made it clear that childhood is not something to be found within children, but within the larger society in which they exist; it denotes the context within which society's newborns develop into "autonomous" members. From this point of view, it might be said that the whole field of child development should be regarded as the study of socialization and that the distinction usually made in psychology between "socialization" and the rest of child development fails to take into account the historical fact that "childhood" was invented.

A consequence of this view of a young child with a family is the emphasis placed on the child's freedom *from* external constraints; this view of child development presupposes the primacy of the individual as the building block of society. The prerequisites thought to be essential for developing into an autonomous individual are:

1. the ability to maintain self-control
2. the ability to select one's actions
3. responsibility for one's actions
4. acquisition of knowledge already possessed by adults
5. the ability to differentiate good from evil

Clearly, the main premises of the context of learning are related to the variety-decreasing mechanisms. The norms of society require not only that the variety be decreased, but also that it be decreased by the individual (through self-control). Thus, the individual must know the permitted range of behavior, both good and bad. If an action falls beyond the tolerated range (increased variety), it will be brought within the range by variety-attenuating mechanisms (e.g., education, punishment). The absoluteness of the rules will eventually generate paradoxes as children develop. Situations that contain incoherent and contradictory elements will confront them. Sometimes, such situations may evolve into problems that are serious enough to require professional intervention.

Two systemic principles can be applied to clarify such situations.

PRINCIPLE 1

In order to promote development in a system, increases in variety (number of possible states) should be dealt with by increased variety in the system's regulator.

Generally, the development of an individual from birth to death has been conceptualized as an independent, linear, and unidirectional process. It may not be as appropriate to describe movements in the family system in a similar way, however (Combrinck-Graham, 1985).

In any social system, there are two opposing tendencies. One represents the values of the group (system as a whole); the other, the values of each of the individuals in the system. The coordination of variety is associated with order, uniformity, collective choice, values of the group, heteronomy (externally ruled), and increased organization. The generation of variety is associated with individual values, autonomy (internally ruled) of the individual, choice, and increased complexity. The interdependence of these opposing tendencies generates the process of social development through learning, socialization, organization, and participation. Development within social systems, then, should be conceptualized as a transformation in the direction of increased generation and coordination of variety.

In Figure 1, line A represents the curve of "development" in which increased levels of variety generation (differentiation) are followed by increased levels of coordination of that variety. If the proliferation of variety x_c is associated with low levels of coordination of that variety y_c (as in line C) the social system has a high degree of disorganization. If instead, the system has a high level of coordination y_b and a low level of differentiation x_b (as in line B), it is an "overorganized" system in which variety is coordinated by suppression, unification, and oppression.

It is necessary to absorb a system's variety in order to regulate it. Otherwise, the system becomes unstable. Fundamentally, there are two ways to absorb system variety: (1) attenuation of the variety and (2) amplification of variety in the regulator. For example, a mother tries to put her four children to sleep at the same time each night. The 6-month-old cries because he wants to be fed; the 6-year-old wants her mother to read her a story; the 4-year-old wants to watch TV; and the 3-year-old complains that she is cold. At this point, the system is highly disorganized. The fact that the different

Figure 1 The Curve of Development

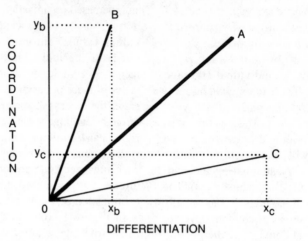

children have different needs at the same time generates a great deal of variety, but the fact that the mother can handle only so many things at once limits the possible coordination. It is necessary either to increase the variety in the system's regulator (e.g., by calling more people to help or by getting the older children to wait), or to decrease the variety in the system (e.g., by enforcing a unifying, armylike rule by which all the children go to the bathroom, brush their teeth, and go to bed at the same time). In both cases, a certain degree of order is achieved, but they differ in the degree of complexity. The latter approach is characterized by a low tolerance for differences, little complexity, and suppression of the development of the individual by the use of vertical (authoritarian) mechanisms of coordination. The former is characterized by a high tolerance for novelty, a great deal of complexity, and developmental variations in the individual by the use of horizontal (participatory) mechanisms of coordination.

In spite of the insistence of society's institutions on the uniqueness of the individual, variety is generally dealt with by attenuation. For example, educational institutions at every level of the hierarchy reduce their variety in three main ways: (1) Teachers constrain the freedom of their students while teachers themselves are simultaneously constrained by the administration. (2) Rigid connections called rules constrain the interactions of the students in the classroom and the staff of the school. (3) The teachers and the administration do not accept arbitrary interference and force those with whom they interact into stereotypes. As previously noted, however, there is another possibility for the regulation of variety, namely, an increase in the variety in the system's regulator.

PRINCIPLE 2

Increases in understanding are believed to be obtainable by expanding the system to be understood.

In practice, the family therapist or consultant must construct problems from elements of the situation that are puzzling, troubling, or uncertain. This process of problem definition requires certain kinds of action that are different from the actions needed in the process of problem solution. The therapist must first create a frame to define a problem so that the problem can later be technically solved. For example, the government of a country in which there is a population explosion calls in a consultant for family planning. In order to transform the situation, which is uncertain and complex in that several intermingled factors are related to the issue, the consultant must first set the problem. After doing the necessary research (e.g., surveys, questionnaires, censuses), the consultant concludes that families' failure to control the number of births is the cause of the population explosion. The problem, as set by the consultant, is the families' ignorance of contraceptive measures. Formulated in this way, the problem can be technically solved, for example, by distributing contraceptives and information on how to use them among the people.

The situation was not presented to the consultant already divided into systems, subsystems, environments, and so on; it was the consultant who began reducing it to something that was manageable by isolating some elements from the field of experience and excluding them from the rest of the experiential field. That very act defined the system under consideration, and the rest of the experiential field became the "environment." So, the actions selected and performed (e.g., selection of questionnaires, population surveys), created a frame within which fertility control was the main parameter. Problem setting is then a process in which, interactively, practitioners name the things that they will make relevant and frame the context in which they will focus their attention.

After waiting the necessary time, the consultant realizes that the intervention was unsuccessful and that the country's birth rate has increased even more. The consultant may blame the failure on an inadequate performance of the intervention and insist on the same intervention, but performed more effectively. On the other hand, the consultant may reanalyze the whole problem, including its formulation. The consultant may collect different kinds of data (e.g., history of the country, economic growth, distribution of newborns according to family income) and find that families have some control over the birth rate because they are having significantly fewer children than it is biologically possible for them to have. Within this new frame, the problem changes, focusing on the reasons that families decide to have a specific number of children. Through the process of problem setting, the system is expanded.

By thus expanding the system and examining it as a network of interrelated factors, the consultant may find that, in the last 50 years, the adult's expected length of life has increased, while the span of employable life remains the same. Therefore, having children is a way of planning for financial security during the periods of unemployment. There may be some other interconnected factors. If, for example, it is much easier in that country for men to find employment, families that have had only daughters may continue having children until they have two or more sons. If the mortality rate is high among children and five children are needed, it will be necessary to have more than five children to ensure that five will survive. Within this expanded frame, the consultant achieves a new level of understanding and recommends interventions that are significantly different from the first (e.g., unemployment insurance, old age security).

The principle of expansionism has a major effect on the way therapists try to set and solve problems. Problem solving is always embedded in problem setting; no problem is treated in isolation, but each problem is formulated as one set of interrelated problems that is treated as a whole. Much of "problem solving" is often symptom suppression and/or removal of deficiencies in the system. Efforts to remove deficiencies are not without success (although there is a risk of treating the wrong problem), but there is an alternative approach that should be considered: adding something, rather than subtracting something. Therapists tend to look for solutions where they find the problem, instead of first setting the problem. Symptoms do not necessarily appear at the site of the cause, however. They may appear in any part of a system, whatever their source. The effort to deal with sets of interacting problems as a whole should be the focus of problem setting, not problem solving.

CASE HISTORIES

Sandra, aged 10, began to have problems 2 years ago. At the end of first grade, the teacher noticed some problems in the way Sandra was reading and contacted the mother, who at that time was in individual therapy for anxiety. The mother mentioned Sandra's problems to her therapist, who immediately suggested that she bring Sandra in for an evaluation of her problem. After the intake session, psychological and psychiatric evaluations were recommended. Following these procedures, it was decided that Sandra would undergo individual therapy with a child therapist. After 6 months of therapy, Sandra's problems had increased. Not only was she having more difficulties in reading, but also she had begun to have severe headaches. The increase in problems led to a concomitant increase in the amount of therapy. The therapist saw Sandra more frequently and included meetings with both Sandra and her mother. At the end of second grade, the teacher decided that Sandra was so far behind that she had to repeat the grade. While repeating the second grade, Sandra performed so poorly that a school team decided to place her in a special class. After a few months, Sandra was still not learning. Furthermore, her headaches had increased in intensity and frequency, and she was occasionally somewhat confused at school.

Ron, aged 11, began to have problems 3 years ago. While he was in third grade, his teacher noted that he had begun to have problems in many academic subjects. The school team decided to place Ron in a special class. After 1½ years, Ron's problems had increased. He was more isolated from his peers, avoided any interactions with them, and wanted to relate only with the adults at school (e.g., teacher, counselor, principal), and suffered from insomnia. Ron's mother, who was in individual psychotherapy, mentioned her son's problems to her therapist, and the therapist suggested that Ron be seen for an intake evaluation. Following the evaluation, it was decided that Ron would receive individual therapy. After 7 months of therapy, the problems had increased even more. The therapist and the counselor suggested that Ron's mother and older brother talk to Ron and try "to make him understand," but the problems continued. One day, Ron threatened to commit suicide while he was at school. At this point, the counselor recommended a psychiatric evaluation for Ron.

Analysis of the Cases

Both children were sent for an evaluation because of "learning problems," but both had acquired additional symptoms (e.g., severe headaches and confusion in Sandra's case and suicide threats and insomnia in Ron's case). After a detailed and careful interview, it was clear that the symptoms in both children were triggered by the inability to maintain good academic performance. Both children were described as very "good"; they had no behavioral problems either at school or at home. In fact, both were "model" children as described by their mothers.

Both mothers believed that the problem originated in past events. Ron's mother explained that the problem was caused by the fact that, when Ron was 18 months old, phimosis had made it necessary to widen the preputial orifice by surgical incision. Similarly, Sandra's mother explained that Sandra had become dehydrated when she was

3 years old (there was no complication to her illness). Her mother also stated that she had a great aunt who is "crazy."

In Figure 2 we can see the stages and the loops involved in the generation of the symptoms that both children presented at the time of the consult.

Let us start our analysis with the problem that both children presented at the very beginning, namely a decrease in academic performance. This had a "triggering" effect on the school team ($+1$). The school team acted to try to solve the problem by placing the children in a special class with the hope of correcting their deficiencies. The actions that were supposed to have an effect on the performance (-2) functioned as a positive loop because of the peers' teasing. This unexpected outcome produced an unforeseen consequence that the children obviously found very distasteful. In addition it created further problems for the children.

The first attempted solution was implemented by the school team. They placed the children in special education classes in spite of the fact that the factors responsible for their poor academic performance were unknown. During the consultation session, the therapist found that both children had been teased by their peers and, in one case, a sibling, as well, for being "retarded" when they were placed in a special class and for being "crazy" when they had to start therapy. Although they had not revealed this previously, both of them felt even more confused and upset because their friends were making fun of them after they were sent to "the psychologist."

This unexpected outcome created further problems for the children. They found it more difficult to perform

Figure 2 Stages and Loops Involved in the Generation of Symptoms

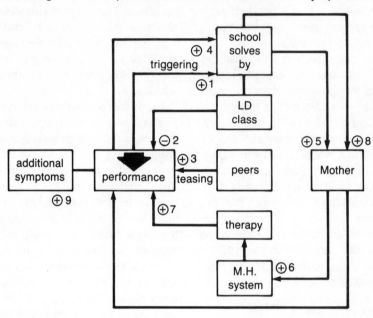

because they felt anxious and angry, but they also felt that they had to demonstrate to the school personnel and their peers that they really "could make it." With time, their performance deteriorated even more. Perceiving that there was nothing else they could do, the school teams started to pressure the mothers (+ 5) to become more involved. Both mothers were already involved with the mental health system (+ 6) which was offering what they could offer—therapy (+ 7). This created a new loop between the children and the peers, who teased the children not only for being "stupid" but also "crazy." Their performance not only remained low, but the children started presenting stress-related symptoms (i.e., headaches, withdrawal, insomnia, anger, irritability and failure to concentrate). Following this, the school team (+ 8) and the therapeutic

system added more pressure on the mothers to become involved. In both cases family therapy was started and the mothers became involved in trying to solve their children's problems (+ 9).

The therapists responsible for the cases first had strongly recommended that both mothers become more involved with their children (e.g., by helping them with their homework). After 6 months, however, the development of the "additional" symptoms motivated the therapists, in agreement with the school's teams, to ask for a psychiatric evaluation.

The consultants for the psychiatric evaluation first examined the premises under which the helpers were acting. The premises were related to the concept of childhood and the context that such a concept imposes. Within this context, the helpers were obviously trying to teach the children to choose, to become autonomous beings, and to know the difference between good and bad. That is the function of education. A consideration of the possibility that this premise may not be correct under all circumstances, however, may lead to the "wrong" questions that produce the "right" answers. If "development" means "to evolve the possibilities of" (i.e., to increase variety), why should children be regulated by methods that restrict and block their development? Increases in variety should be dealt with by an increase of variety in the regulators. This requires an increase in understanding (i.e., an expansion of the system to be understood).

Simply by asking the children what they wanted, the consultant shifted the whole context. It became apparent that the attempted solutions had become the problem. There are at least two possible ways of dealing with this: changing the intended solutions or changing the problem itself by resetting it and trying to fit the situation to the new frame. The problem of these children was reset. Within the new frame, the problem was no longer why these children were not learning, but why should they have to learn?

After the new frame had been set, both children became very interested, talkative, and active during the session. Sandra revealed that she was not very interested in school and that her dream was to be a housewife. She wanted to learn to cook, to iron, to do the shopping, and to do all the chores in the house. She enjoyed helping her mother with the housework. She was going to school because her mother expected her to be a nurse, something her mother always wanted to be. Like Sandra, Ron was not

interested in school. He wanted to be a professional dancer, and was going to school only because his mother wanted him to be a social worker. The children's mothers reponded by saying that the children did not know what was good for them; they were "too small."

Further inquiry showed that both mothers were under a considerable amount of stress. Both were divorced. Sandra's mother had three other children; Ron's mother had two. Both Sandra and Ron played a central role in the family. Sandra helped her mother with the chores, and Ron helped his mother by looking after his two younger sisters. Both Sandra and Ron were extremely concerned about their mothers and felt that they were the cause of their mothers' suffering. They both missed school to help their mothers at home, and their mothers were proud of them trying to help; however, they were punished at school for the same actions, because missing school was irresponsible.

When the school and the therapist began pressuring the mothers to become more involved, each mother threatened to punish her child severely if the child's performance at school did not improve. At this point, the additional symptoms appeared. Both children were confused by the fact that they had to wait "to grow up" (i.e., to be able to make choices for themselves), because in other instances they were expected to act grown up already (i.e., to help their mothers at home). As Alice put it, "Being so many different sizes in a day is very confusing."

Interventions

In Sandra's case, the consultant informed the family that during the

2 years of therapy an incorrect problem had been addressed and that was probably the reason why the therapeutic efforts, although very well intentioned, had had no results. Sandra had been confused and unable to decide between learning the "stuff" at school or the "stuff" at home. At the end of the session, the consultant made the following statements:

> So, for the next 3 weeks, if Mother wants to help, she has to concentrate on helping her daughter discover what running a house means, because she is an expert at that. But Mother should absolutely forget about helping Sandra with her homework or anything that has to do with school. Sandra is going to experience school by herself, with only the regular help that all kids get. As for the rest of Sandra's helpers, psychologists and counselors are excellent at helping children with learning problems, but not children with indecision problems.

Three weeks later, Sandra informed the consultant that she had decided to continue in school and to learn about housekeeping when her mother was free to teach her. Her headaches and confusion had completely disappeared, and she was not so concerned with her peers' opinions about her.

In Ron's case, the consultant met with the therapist, school counselor, teacher, and family in order to explain the situation to them. The consultant suggested that family therapy continue to discover a way to extricate Ron from the erratic situation without suicide.

CONCLUSIONS

At the time that these cases were referred to the consultant, different professionals had already tried to solve the problems. All the helpers operated under the assumption that all children must have a formal education. They believed the problem to be a deficiency in the learning process that had to be corrected. Their approach was to try to remove the symptom by providing specialized education, by increasing the intensity of the input (i.e., requiring more hours of education), and by referring the child for therapeutic intervention for the emotional aspects.

The consultant found that these children were very curious, had interests in several areas (e.g., sports, soap operas, housekeeping), and had been learning about these things for the past several years in a nonformal way. The consultant reset the problem, shifting the focus from a learning deficiency to the reason for a formal education. As a result of resetting the problem, the context expanded; the problem and the interventions took a different form. The interventions were aimed at increasing the variety in the system regulators (e.g., teachers, counselors, mothers, therapist) by generating a new way of dealing with the "unique case," thus allowing for the actualization of the potential variety within the child.

> This reminds us of an anecdote in which E.F. Schumacher was seated in a restaurant next to a family of three—mother, father, and a young boy of 8 or 9 years. They all examined the menu in the presence of the waitress. The boy said that he wanted liver and bacon. The father studied the menu, as did the boy's mother; then, the father ordered three steaks. The waitress repeated the order, "Two steaks; one liver and bacon," and departed. The boy looked at his mother and said, "Mommy, she thinks I'm real!"

If the participants in such systems are successful in matching the increased variety with an increase in the complexity of the coordination of that variety, they all move to a higher level of development where the contradictions that were generated in the previous level of development will dissolve. This approach may be useful in a variety of situations for the treatment of children and their families. Furthermore, therapeutic interventions can be understood within a wider context. For example, the therapeutic technique of "empowering parents" can be understood as a technique that disrupts contradictory rules rather than one that simply gives parents authority over their children. The essential point is that children and their families are often caught in a deadlock of contradictions in which the child is both "coming and going of age." The possibility of breaking such a deadlock is enhanced if the child can be helped either to "grow up" or to "grow down."

REFERENCES

Aries, P. (1962). *Centuries of childhood: A social history of family life*. New York: Vintage Books.

Combrinck-Graham, L. (1985). A developmental model for family systems. *Family Process, 24*(2), 139–150.

3

Family Treatment for Childhood Anxiety Disorders

Lee Combrinck-Graham, MD
Director, Master of Family Therapy
  Program
Mental Health Sciences
Hahnemann University
Philadelphia, Pennsylvania

MOST THERAPISTS WHO work in settings where children are the identified patients have been trained to think of children in isolation from their families. Family therapists who work with children must understand children's problems in the context of the family, however. The family therapist almost invariably begins the exploration of a child's difficulties by examining the nuclear family (i.e., everyone living in the household). The family becomes the patient.

When a distressing symptom, such as anxiety, first appears in a child, a traditionally trained child therapist focuses on the inner conflicts that are being manifested in the symptom. In contrast, a family therapist's first interest is the context in which the symptom occurs, such as the family, the school, extended family, or other relevant social system. Furthermore, the family therapist is interested in the historical contexts, including what was happening in the life of the family when the symptoms began, what is happening in the family when the symptom is expressed, and what are the responses of the family members when the symptom appears. Within these contexts, the family therapist searches for patterns of interpersonal interaction that make it possible to understand and intervene in the family system.

When a child experiences anxiety, the child's distress calls attention to the problem. Not only is anxiety real and painful for the child, but also it may interfere with normal developmental experiences for the child. For example, separation anxiety interferes with a child's schooling and peer relationships. From the viewpoint of a family therapist, the problem does not originate within the child, however, but rather resonates within the family system. For the family therapist, working with the family system is the most effective way to alleviate the child's discomfort and to get the child back on track developmentally.

The family therapist's first explorations focus on the family's experience of the problem. In addition to the questions mentioned earlier about events in the family when the problem developed, the therapist may ask

- What happens when family members discuss the problem among themselves or with the child?
- How have they dealt with the school about the problem?
- Whom have they consulted?
- How do they feel about the advice that they have been given?

With such questions, the family systems investigator draws larger and larger circles around the child and the child's symptoms to include the response patterns at larger and larger system levels (e.g., family, school, health care system).

In raising these questions with the whole family, the therapist seeks information at a variety of levels. The first, of course, is the level of *facts*. When the therapist asks each family member his or her experience of the issue, however, the differences among the reported experiences become apparent; there are many ways to view facts within families. As the varying viewpoints provide information for the family therapist, the second level of information is *difference*. The third level as observed by the family therapist is *behavior*. In order to enrich the data at this level, the therapist may

request an enactment, saying simply, "Show me what you do." At the fourth level of information, the therapist seeks to discover relevant, repetitive *patterns* in the interpersonal activity that surrounds the problem. It is believed that the problem plays a role in the repetition of such patterns, which are manifested in expanding areas of functioning in the individual, symptomatic child in the intergenerational relationship of the parents' families of origin, and in the interaction between the family and society. Although different family therapists may focus on different areas, changing these relationship patterns is the goal of family therapy.

THE FAMILY AS A CONTEXT FOR ANXIETY

Family therapists believe that all symptoms occur in an interpersonal context. In the specific instance of anxiety symptoms, Minuchin, Baker, and Rosman (1978) assessed the mediation of stress in families of brittle diabetic children by using free fatty acids (FFAs) as markers for changes in the level of stress. Measuring FFAs at 15-minute intervals, they found an elevated level of FFAs both in the children who were observing a parental conflict through the one-way mirror and in the parents who were having the argument. When the children were brought into the room with the parents, the level of FFAs gradually decreased in the parents and in the nonpsychosomatic children; however, in each family the level of FFAs in the symptomatic (brittle diabetic) child remained elevated for some time after the experiment had been terminated. The interpersonal behavior that coincided with these shifts in the measurements of physiologic stress was the intrusion of the symptomatic child into the parental argument. The child attempted to mediate, took one parent's side to unbalance and finish the argument, or drew negative attention to him or herself in such a way that the parental conflict was forgotten. This experiment was an elegant illustration of family-mediated stress, showing that people are exquisitely responsive to one another even at the biochemical level.

It is clear that the child who experiences the anxiety has the increased pulse rate, the sleep problem, the diaphoresis, the sense of foreboding, and the excessive worry. Because the experience of the child relates to the experience of the family, however, as a consequence and as a cause, it must be understood as part of a recursive process. Breaking these recursive patterns so that the family can form new, more functional patterns is the swiftest and most lasting effective intervention for these problems.

Family therapy requires more than simply talking to all the family members. Freud's classic case of Little Hans (1909), in which the father treated the child under the supervision of Freud, was not family therapy, because the family relationship system was not the focus either of the hypothesis about the cause of the child's problem or of the treatment. Nowhere, for example, is there a discussion of how the father dealt with his wife's threats to cut off the child's "widdler" if he continued to masturbate. A family therapist might guess that the father's role in the treatment brought him closer to the boy, moving him from a relatively peripheral to a more central parenting position in the family. Thus, although it might be said that the family

changed as a result of the treatment, that was certainly not the intent of the treatment.

Haley (1976) described family therapy for a childhood phobia in a case entitled, "A Modern Little Hans." In this case, a youngster's fear of dogs was understood as part of the pattern of family relationships. In addition to the child's symptoms and a parenting arrangement in which the mother was involved and competent while the father was uninvolved, marital difficulties in the parents were part of the pattern. The therapy was designed to change the relationship patterns, thus removing the boy and his symptoms from the focus of the parents in the system.

FAMILY ASSESSMENT AND TREATMENT FOR CHILDHOOD ANXIETY DISORDERS

With most family systems, assessment and treatment are indistinguishable from one another. The therapist's understanding of the problem evolves from observations of the family's responses to a series of probes that can have therapeutic results. The very presence of the family in the therapist's office is a probe that elicits informative behavior from the family members. Their awareness of themselves as an interacting system is altered when they look at themselves through the lens of the therapist's inquiry.

The first encounter between the therapist and the family is not a random approach of "go with the flow." Usually, the therapist has some information about the family—at least the age of the identified patient and the chief complaint. Even with a minimal amount of advance information, the therapist has "prejudices" about the family that, made explicit, may become working hypotheses. In the case of children with anxiety disorders, the therapist may hypothesize that the family system provides insufficient reassurance for the child and may spend the first session looking for evidence that supports this hypothesis or suggests another. For example, the therapist may find that the parents become uncomfortable during discussions of the child's experience, want to turn the child over to the therapist, are intimidated by the emotional expressions of the child, or subtly request reassurance from the child.

Having found some support for the hypothesis, the therapist then learns more about the child's role in maintaining the pattern, perhaps by specifically asking one parent to take charge of comforting the child. The parent may be clumsy at comforting, demonstrating uncertainty with the youngster. In addition, however, the therapist may observe that the child shrugs off the parent's efforts to provide comfort. This interaction—child becoming anxious, parent attempting to offer support, child not being receptive and, therefore, not being comforted and continuing to be anxious—represents a sequence that may occur frequently when the child experiences symptoms. Furthermore, if there are two parents, the parent who is not directly involved in the task becomes a critical onlooker, and that parent's judgment is also a part of the anxiety sequence.

The hypothesis of inadequate reassurance may be extended to a lack of parental sureness. Thus, one parent may order the child who refuses to go to

school to get dressed, while the other worries about whether the child is well enough to go to school. The child receives a mixed message, the meaning of which is not clear. When the therapist asks the family to "show me how it goes when he has his stomachaches in the morning," the family demonstrates its distinctive versions of these processes.

Parents may also lack confidence in dealing with the staff at their children's school. They may feel overwhelmed by the expertise of the teachers and counselors; this feeling may be manifested in the presence of the therapist as well. Thus, anxiety disorders may occur in children whose family support systems are themselves inadequately supported. A parent with little self-confidence, for example, may not be receiving support from the other parent, the extended family, or school personnel. Furthermore, the child therapist who is too expert in handling the child may contribute to the problem in kind.

The origin of the parents' lack of sureness may forever remain a mystery—one that is not of great importance to the family therapist. Further probing is likely to reveal, however, that the parents have experienced (and are now experiencing) a similar lack of firm reassurance from other people in their lives, such as their own parents, their peers, and their employers. Frequently, these individuals seek help because of their lack of confidence, but they may receive only authoritative advice that confirms their need to seek it. They become part of a system of revolving insecurities in which seeking reassurance leads to more insecurity; this system will come to include their children and may be expressed through the children's anxiety.

If the therapist finds some validity in the hypothesis that family interaction is related to the symptoms, the general treatment goal will be to disrupt the symptomatic cycle, especially by restoring parental competence and confidence. This can be done through a variety of exercises. For example, parents can be coached to conduct a parent-teacher meeting in which they offer some expertise as parents (Combrinck-Graham & Higley, 1984). If a grandmother is reported to be the critical factor, the therapist may work with her and encourage her to step aside so that appropriate parental authority can be established. The therapist will work at whatever levels of the system seem most accessible and use as many approaches as indicated. Throughout this process, the therapist elicits parents' opinions about the treatment, acknowledging their greater familiarity and expertise with their own children.

SEPARATION ANXIETY DISORDER: TREATMENT

(The following case was abstracted from the *DSM-III Case Book* (Spitzer, Skodol, Gibbon, and Williams, 1981), pp. 167–168.) The treatment described demonstrates the family therapist's approach and some possible scenarios.

Michael is 7½ years old, the older of two boys from a two-parent family. The initial complaint is that he does not sleep in his own bed. He falls asleep in his parents' bed and is then put into his own bed in a room he shares with his 5-year-old brother, but he always finds his way back to his parents' room by morning. If they again put him back in his bed, they find him huddled by their bedroom door. This pattern began when Michael was 2 years old and started having tantrums at bedtime.

In addition, Michael has begun to complain of physical symptoms, such as stomachaches and headaches, on school mornings. He often complains that he is going to die and should be taken to the hospital. He is beginning to refuse to go to school, because the idea of leaving home in the morning terrifies him. His school performance is fine.

Even before seeing the family, a family therapist begins by developing some hypotheses. In this case, the hypotheses may be as follows:

1. The sleep problem began around the time of the younger brother's birth and could be associated with the parents'

- preoccupation with the new baby, which led to sibling rivalry and made it necessary for Michael to define his place in their affections.

- concern about Michael's feelings about the new baby which led them to indulge him by inviting him into bed with them rather than establishing reassuring limits about bedtime (that is, maintaining consistency for him in the face of change in the family). This indulgence may also occur because the preoccupation of Michael's mother with the baby has excluded the father, who then directs his attention to Michael.

2. The school problem may be developing because

- the younger brother is beginning school, leaving the parents with two school-aged children and an early empty nest. Michael fills this nest if he stays home with a stomachache. It may be discovered that the parents are arguing about whether to have another baby.

- the mother may have started working now that both children are in school, and there may be some conflict about this. Perhaps the father wants her to be home, and in his old coalition with Dad, Michael makes mornings difficult for them.

3. In general, Michael's parents are not in charge of bedtime or school attendance. Michael is in charge, but unable to manage. Such power in a small person results in anxiety—and willfulness.

In the next stage, the therapist assesses the family system to explore the validity and usefulness of the hypotheses. The whole family, including the younger brother, Kevin, is invited to attend a session.

Kevin immediately finds the toys and busies himself with them while Michael sits down between his parents, all three looking expectantly at the therapist. "Who can tell me what the problem is?" the therapist asks. There is silence; then the father starts to speak, but the mother interrupts. She explains their concerns about Michael. She says that he is upset, does not get enough sleep, and gets these terrible stomachaches. She cannot believe that there is nothing physically wrong with him. The father says that the mother is soft on Michael and wonders how she explains his lack of stomachaches on

weekends. Michael says that he does not know what the matter is, but he gets scared at night and his stomach hurts. Kevin volunteers that Mike can sleep in his bed because he is not scared, and Michael scowls. Kevin adds that he loves school, but Michael has a mean teacher and a lot of hard work to do.

The therapist continues, "Tell me about bedtime for the boys. What time do they go to bed? Who puts them to bed? What routines are there?" The parents reply that the mother puts the boys to bed, because the father gets them too "worked up." She reminds the boys of bedtime about 15 minutes beforehand, and they take a quick bath and hop into bed. They do not have a story read to them, because they like to watch TV until the last minute. They have the same bedtime.

The therapist asks about the morning. "Show me what goes on at home when you get up in the morning." The therapist asks Kevin to pretend that he is Michael and then asks the family to proceed. "What time does it start? Who wakes up the boys?" Kevin begins with a dramatic groan, but the parents are slow to start the enactment.

"Who begins?" asks the therapist.

Dad says, "Come on, Mike, get dressed and get all ready. Get some breakfast into you; then you'll feel better."

"OK," says Kevin.

"Is that what Mike does?" asks the therapist.

"No," says Kevin, who then begins more moaning.

Mother says, "Try to get dressed now."

"No-o-o-o!" moans Kevin, falling to the floor and grasping his stomach. Everyone starts to laugh, except Michael, who is angry and sullen. The therapist asks what happens next, and they answer that Dad gets angry and Mom gets more concerned.

"How does it end?"

Dad takes Kevin to school, while Mom soothes Mike, who does eventually get dressed, although slowly. She takes him to school, where he arrives late and without breakfast. She then goes to work; she, too, is late.

The therapist asks Michael, "Did Kevin do a good job being you?"

"No," says Michael, "I don't make that much noise."

"You do, too," says Kevin.

The therapist asks the parents whether they want to begin with the sleep problem or the stomach problem. The mother wants to start with the sleep problem, because she thinks lack of sleep gives Michael a stomachache. The father wants to start with the stomach problem, however, because it upsets everyone's day. The therapist asks the parents to decide between themselves. They have a brief discussion, and the father gives in to the mother, even though he does not agree with her. The therapist commends them on reaching a decision, reviews their description of the problem and the bedtime routine, and says, "What could you change, here?"

The session ends with the assignment of a task for the parents: to determine what changes they could

make in the bedtime routine. It is suggested that nothing be done to change the morning routine until the sleep problem is under control.

After the first session, the therapist reviews and refines the hypotheses in light of the experience with the family:

1. The problem developed around the birth of Kevin. Michael does not have a good relationship with his brother and is not differentiated as a child from his parents. He is much too much involved with them. This is seen in Michael's attention to his parents and the therapist, in contrast to Kevin's early ability to occupy himself and his objective "playing" of the Michael role.

2. The parents are on different sides of the issue and are not sure what to do. They keep arguing, and they keep failing to solve the problems.

In asking the parents to decide which problem to deal with the therapist has already begun to implement the treatment plan. It is part of an effort to have the parents make decisions together. The therapist accepts both the decision and the decision-making process, even though it is not a true consensus; the therapist is more interested in their reaching an agreement than in the way that they do so.

The formal treatment plan includes the following:

1. Whenever possible, ensure that the parents make decisions about the children together.

2. Introduce the concept of differentiation. The fact that Michael is the older brother may help him to find his own

place in the sibship. The therapist will ask the parents to consider setting a different bedtime for Michael, having him go with one parent while the other is with Kevin, and reading him a different story and to decide between themselves the feasibility of these ideas. At first, they may reach a decision that Michael does not like, and they may retreat from it. The therapist will encourage them to pursue their decision, however, and they will be successful.

3. Implement a similar process in regard to the stomachaches, if they persist. They may abate when the parents change their attitudes and feel more competent in managing the children. If the parent-child interaction shifts around bedtime, it is likely to shift around stomachaches, too.

After the family members express their satisfaction with bedtime—the parents with pleasure, Michael with a kind of sheepish acknowledgment, and Kevin with boisterous support of his brother—the therapist asks, "Well, are we ready to work on the stomach problem?"

Michael volunteers, "I don't have stomachaches anymore." The therapist is incredulous. "Not even one a week? Not even a little twinge—you know what a twinge is, don't you?"

The question of symptom substitution is often raised when there is a rapid resolution of symptoms. Not only is symptom substitution unlikely when the disappearance of symptoms accompanies a real shift in family functioning, however, but also other, unaddressed

symptoms may disappear (Combrinck-Graham, 1974).

Michael insists that he has no more stomachaches. The therapist turns helplessly to the parents. "This is serious. I'm concerned that Michael has given up all his symptoms so quickly, because he may be relieving you of the task of negotiating with each other about the best way to take care of him. For this reason, I want you to pretend that Michael has a stomachache in the morning and to consider the problems that you had to deal with when he really did have a stomachache. This means that you must have a discussion about whether he should get dressed, whether he should eat breakfast, and whether he will be ready to leave for school on time. I don't, for a minute, want you to think that being agreeable parents is easy. And, Michael, if you could just pretend to have a stomachache one or two mornings this week, I think that will really help your parents to do their job. OK?"

Everyone thinks this is silly. The therapist asks Michael to demonstrate how he would act if he were pretending to have a stomachache. Not nearly as reticent as he was in the first session, he gives a fine performance. "That's great," says the therapist. "That way your parents will really have a job trying to figure out what to do."

The parents enjoy the game and promise to be really mean the next time that Michael complains of a stomachache. "But, remember," warns the therapist, "Michael really does have stomachaches. He didn't just make them up, though I hope he will make up a few in the next week or two so that you won't forget the problems they cause."

By "restraining" (Haley, 1976) the family from changing too rapidly, the therapist attempts to deal with the "flight into health" phenomenon. In this case, for example, Michael could be accommodating his parents, making it appear that things are better even though no real change has occurred. Usually, families carry out the task assigned and have a hilarious tale to tell about their experiences. This family's old pattern of the stomachache and the troubles in getting Michael to school is likely to become a somewhat beloved family story to be retold on cozy winter evenings. "Re-

member when you and Daddy used to fight about whether I should go to school?" queries Michael. . . .

The total treatment time for such a case is approximately six sessions. It could be longer, however, if the parents find it difficult to reach decisions between themselves or if the child is able to deter them from implementing their decisions, for example.

Michael remains fine. In the Spring, he starts Little League. He drinks a big glass of milk for breakfast each day because his idol, Mike Schmidt, does. Kevin is complaining about Michael's privileges. The therapist asks the parents, "Do you know how to handle that?"

"Yes," they reply.

REFERENCES

Combrinck-Graham, L. (1974). Structural family therapy in psychosomatic illness: Therapy of anorexia nervosa and asthma. *Clinical Pediatrics, 13,* 827–833.

Combrinck-Graham, L., & Higley, L.W. (1984). Working with families of school-aged handicapped children. In E.I. Coppersmith (Ed.), *Families with handicapped members* (pp. 18–29). Rockville, MD: Aspen Publishers, Inc.

Freud, S. (1909). Analysis of a phobia in a five-year-old boy. In *The sexual enlightenment of*

children. New York: Crowell-Collier Publishing Company, 1963.

Haley, J. (1976). *Problem-solving therapy.* San Francisco: Jossey-Bass.

Minuchin, S., Baker, L., & Rosman, B.L. (1978). *Psychosomatic families.* Cambridge, MA and London: Harvard University Press.

Spitzer, R.L., Skodol, A.E., Gibbon, M., & Williams, J.B.W. (Eds.). (1981). *DSM-III case book.* Washington, DC: American Psychiatric Association, pp. 167–168.

4

Elective Mutism in Families with Young Children

Marion Lindblad-Goldberg, PhD
Associate Professor of Clinical
  Psychiatry
    and
Director, Family Therapy Center
University of Cincinnati College of
  Medicine
Cincinnati, Ohio

Once upon a time there was a girl who had never seen her father look anything but sad. At last she asked him about his sadness. He told her that one day in his wicked anger he had cast a spell over her three brothers and turned them into ravens.

From this moment onwards the girl could not rest at home and so she set out to look for her brothers. When she had found them, she asked what she could do to set them free. "It would be a hard task," they said. "You must not speak a word for three years, for if you do we shall be ravens for the rest of our lives. Besides this, you must not visit us anymore." "I will do it for the love of you," said the girl, and returned home (Muller-Guggenbuhl, 1958, p. 167).

DESPITE THE INCREASING attention given to childhood behavior problems in the family systems model, the family therapy literature contains few discussions of elective mutism in young children. Historically, the refusal to speak has been attributed to the life situation and the emotions of the child. Hence, the symptom has often been perceived as contained within the child, and most research and treatment procedures have focused directly on the child.

Over the years, opinions have differed on both the definition and the classifications of elective mutism (Hayden, 1980). Is it a symptom of an emotional disorder, a specific emotional disorder, or simply a descriptive label (Wilkins, 1985; Young-erman, 1979)? While some have suggested that family pathology is the basis of elective mutism (Bakwin & Bakwin, 1972), only a few examples of clinical work with families have been described in the literature (Browne, Wilson, & Layborune, 1963; Goll, 1979; Meyers, 1984; Pustrom & Speers, 1964; Rosenberg & Lindblad, 1978). Even so, it is now possible to delineate the characteristics of families with young electively mute children and develop a conceptual model that will aid in family treatment.

DEFINITION AND INCIDENCE OF ELECTIVE MUTISM

Originally termed aphasia voluntaria by the German physician Kussmaul, selective nonverbal behavior without an obvious cause is most commonly referred to as elective mutism (Tramer, 1934). This term excludes organic or functional forms of mutism. Elective mutes can and do speak normally, but they restrict their conversation to certain people and specific settings. Typically, the electively mute child speaks naturally to one (often the mother) or both parents, to siblings, and sometimes to other relatives who live in the home. There have been rare cases in which a child talks only to outsiders—not to the parents.

The electively mute child most frequently refuses to talk to those outside the home or at school. The mutism and social withdrawal is more severe with peers than with adults in all situations outside the home. The child's age at onset in reported cases ranges from 3.7 years to 14 years, with a mean age of 6.1 years. The duration of the mutism in these cases ranges from 7 months to 9 years, with a mean of 5.1 years (Wilkins, 1985).

According to parents' descriptions, the electively mute child becomes unusually shy when away from home or in the company of acquaintances or relatives beyond the immediate family. The problem is not generally identified until the child enters nursery school or kindergarten, however. Frequently, the child resists entering the classroom unless led into it and shows little desire to partici-

pate in classroom activities. Some children have been described as negativistic, emotionally immature, and aggressive at home.

Transient mutism is not unusual for children who are entering school, particularly for immigrant children (Bradley & Sloman, 1975), but more than 90% of these adjustment reactions improve spontaneously over the first school year (Brown & Lloyd, 1975). Persistent elective mutism is rare; an incidence of 0.8/1,000 seven-year-old children was found in one British study (Fundudis, Kolvin, & Garside, 1979).

CHARACTERISTICS OF ELECTIVELY MUTE CHILDREN AND THEIR FAMILIES

Most of the information available on the characteristics of electively mute children and their families is contained in single case descriptions or small-sample studies that had no control groups. In a few studies, groups of electively mute children have been compared with matched control groups of either children who are speech-retarded (Kolvin & Fundudis, 1981) or children who have other emotional disorders (Wilkins, 1985).

Characteristics of the Electively Mute Child

Although the intelligence of electively mute children varies widely, the mean IQ scores reported are in the lower ranges (i.e., 85 to 100.3) (Friedman & Karagan, 1973). Elective mutism is more common in girls than in boys (Wright, 1968). Studies on the significance of birth order have conflicting results.

Many researchers have reported that a trauma, such as a mouth injury and/or mouth punishment, the birth of a sibling, a death in the immediate family, or separation from the mother, occurred when the children were in the stage of speech development (Hesselman, 1973; Parker, Olsen, & Throckmorton, 1960). There are strong indications that some speech problems may have occurred before the onset of mutism, but no hearing problems have been found. Many electively mute children have been bedwetters or soilers. Some researchers have reported electroencephalogram abnormalities.

The characteristics of the electively mute child most commonly mentioned in the literature are shyness away from home, aggression, sulkiness, stubbornness, manipulativeness, negativism, strong-willed attitudes at home, depression, immaturity, anxiety, and excessive and unusual motor activity (Wergeland, 1979).

Characteristics of the Families of Elective Mutes

The majority of the families of electively mute children have a two-parent structure. Family size, number of children in the family, and socioeconomic status are not differentiating factors. The families have been described as socially isolated, suspicious, and fearful of the outside world. One or both parents usually exhibit limited speech patterns and social reticence. Occasionally, siblings have such characteristics as well. This suggests that the family unit boundary is often rigid and closed, tending to shut out the external world. Several case histories suggest that the family has implicit rules that prohibit disclosure of the family "secrets" outside the family.

There is frequently profound disharmony and unresolved tension in these families, although separation or divorce is uncommon. Wives are described as shy, depressed, and unable to express anger, while husbands are reported to be aggressive, quick-tempered, or indifferent. As parents, these couples tend to be split; the mothers are overprotective and spoil the child, and the fathers either dominate by sternness or corporal punishment, or assume a peripheral, passive role with the child. Some cases of alcoholism in the fathers have been reported.

The mother-child relationship has been the most emphasized and studied. In this extremely overinvolved dyad, there is a reciprocal process in which the more the mother responds to and for the child, the more the child demands of the mother and refuses to respond to others.

AN OPEN SYSTEMS MODEL OF ELECTIVE MUTISM

Like the model developed by Minuchin and his associates (1975) to describe psychosomatic illness in children, the open systems model of elective mutism (depicted in Figure 1) emphasizes the feedback processes between elective mutes and their context. It is postulated that (1) the family's organization and relationship to its extrafamilial context is closely related to the development and maintenance of elective mutism in children, and (2) the elective mute's refusal to speak plays a major role in maintaining family homeostasis.

Four factors operate simultaneously in the development of elective mutism in children. First, the child is developmentally vulnerable. Second, the child's family has four structural characteristics:

Figure 1 An Open Systems Model of Elective Mutism

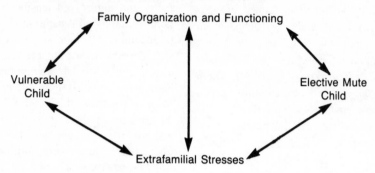

Source: From Minuchin, S., Rosman, B., & Baker, L. *Psychosomatic Families*. Cambridge, MA and London: Harvard University Press, 1978, p. 21.

(1) enmeshment, (2) overprotectiveness, (3) lack of conflict resolution and role of the elective mute, and (4) rigidity. Third, the elective mute's role in the family's pattern of conflict avoidance reinforces the symptom. Fourth, the family experiences a developmental crisis whenever it reaches a point in the family life cycle that requires an increased exchange between the family and the extrafamilial environment.

Vulnerability

The electively mute child is born into a family in which the unspoken needs and tensions of the family members have led them to believe that there is safety in silence and distance from the extrafamilial environment. Maternal silence caused by depression and/or intergenerational modeling characterizes the attachment process. "Alone with mother, the young child is safe and talks; when strangers appear, the infant stops moving and the child stops talking" (Youngerman, 1979, p. 284). Any trauma experienced by the child during the period of

language development strengthens the "safety in silence" response.

Because both talking and toileting reflect the family's, particularly the mother's, difficulties with socialization, not talking and not toileting become the mode of experiencing the world whenever the child is away from the mother. The child's continuing overinvolvement with the mother results in insufficient stimulation of the child's autonomy and verbal communication with others.

Family Transactional Characteristics

Enmeshment and Overprotectiveness

Enmeshment and diffusion of interpersonal boundaries are normal in a child's early relationships; they are magnified in the elective mute's family, however, because the family system has closed its boundaries to the outside world. Under extrafamilial stress, the family closes ranks even further and becomes progressively more enmeshed. Since language is often the bridge between the family's culture and society, it is not surprising that elective mutism develops within this type of family environment.

Implicit family rules that protect family members from the dangers of the outside world evolve as the family's enmeshment becomes more developmentally inappropriate. These rules prohibit discussion of family secrets about such matters as alcoholism, sexuality, criminality, and marital conflict.

Lack of Conflict Resolution; Role of the Elective Mute; and Rigidity

Two patterns of family structure typify the families of electively mute children. In the first, there is a stable coalition between the mother and child, often against the father, and the child's behavior is used to attack the father. In some families, the mother and child may form a coalition against the grandparents or others. This coalition is often the result of the mother's hostility and disappointments in other family members. The mother is timid and afraid of expressing anger toward her husband (or others), because he will punish her either by refusing to talk to her or by becoming abusive to her. From his peripheral position in the presence of a mother-child coalition, the father either becomes passive and indifferent or harsh in his anger toward the child, thus avoiding conflict with the mother.

While the dependence of the child is initially gratifying to the mother, who may have been frequently depressed during the child's early years, feelings become ambivalent in both mother and child as time passes. The child's excessive demands on the mother increase as the child grows older, and, in some instances, the child becomes oppositional and controlling. The mother may resent the child's constant demands, but she continues to cater to and be dominated by the child.

The second frequently occurring pattern also serves to avoid conflict. In this pattern, the conflictual dyad (the two people in conflict, i.e., spouse and or other) unites against extrafamilial stressors or in protective concern for the child when the child begins to move out from the family into the extrafamilial environment.

Developmental Crisis

Enmeshed, closed families have great difficulty when they reach a development point at which it is necessary to decrease the emotional closeness between family members and increase their exchange with the outside world. When the child enters school, for example, the family does not change its accustomed patterns of interaction; instead, the symptom of elective mutism emerges, allowing the family to detour conflict via concern for the child and/or loyalty to the family in reaction to the school's crusade to rescue the child. Often, the school becomes part of the cycle that maintains the child's mutism.

CASE EXAMPLE

Jerry had first gained the attention of an outside agency when, at the age of 3½ years, he had refused to respond verbally for an eye examination at a hospital clinic. The results of a hearing test were normal. He received speech therapy at the hospital, but it was unsuccessful; he was referred to a preschool program. In the following year, he began kindergarten. Jerry used no speech in any of these settings—except when his mother was with him. The consulting psychiatrist for the kindergarten referred Jerry, then 5 years old, for a diagnostic evaluation.

Jerry was living in a two-family house with his unemployed 26-year-old mother, Judy, and his 3-year-old sister, Josephine. His divorced grandfather lived downstairs. Jerry's father had left when his mother was 3 months pregnant and had returned to see Jerry only twice. Judy had married her boyfriend of 2 years, John, aged 35, the week before the referral to the Family Therapy Center. John was divorced and the father of three children; he was reportedly a recovering alcoholic.

Judy and her younger brother, Joe, were raised in a working-class, Catholic, two-parent family in which both parents worked. During Judy's childhood and adolescence, the family moved five times, and the family members grew to depend on each other. Judy's paternal great-grandfather lived with the family for 5 years until his death; at this point, Judy's father had a lengthy psychiatric hospitalization, but it was never discussed in the family. Judy's maternal grandmother joined the household shortly before her paternal great-grandfather's death.

Two years later, following a hysterectomy, Judy's mother became paranoid and negative about her children's social involvements. Judy worried constantly about the defamatory sexual comments that her mother made about her to friends.

After years of marital conflict, the parents divorced when Judy was 15. The secret of her father's homosexuality became public through the court. Judy and Joe lived with their mother for 2 years, then began living with their father. Judy assumed household responsibilities for her father, but could not express the anger that she felt for the entourage of strange men who came to the house.

At 18 years of age, Judy married an emotionally abusive man whom she left after meeting Jerry's father, George, who was living at her father's house. Her pregnancy with Jerry was accidental, and George left her during her 3rd month. She later became pregnant with Josephine by a friend of her brother's. At the time of her daughter's birth, her divorce became final, and she discovered Josephine's father in bed with her own father. She was devastated by the perceived betrayal of her father and became emotionally withdrawn and depressed for almost 2 years.

During her pregnancy with Jerry, Judy had conflicting feelings about keeping the baby, but finally decided to keep him. She breast-fed him for 4 months, but began supplemental bottle feedings when he failed to gain weight. He lost interest in the breast and started gaining. "He didn't cuddle, because he didn't want to be bothered." He spoke single words when he was 15 to 18 months of age, but stopped saying words to anyone except his mother when he was 2 and his sister was born. When his sister started talking at 15 months, Jerry began to put three words together; as she became more articulate, so did he. At the time of referral, he talked only to his mother and sister.

His grandfather was upset and annoyed because Jerry did not talk to him.

Toilet training began when Josephine was born. By the age of 4½, Jerry was trained for stools, but continued to soil. He was separated from his mother when Josephine was born and again 3 months later when a fire damaged their home.

The mother appeared shy and depressed at the evaluation session. Jerry and his mother clung to each other. He was physically awkward, tentative, cautious, and constricted. He became oppositional and withholding when frustrated. He was afraid to be assertive and had a rigid cognitive style. While his IQ on a *Nonverbal Test of Intelligence* was 78, there were indications that he had average potential. His receptive language skills were normal.

TREATMENT APPROACHES

In reviewing the vast array of interventions that have been used to persuade the electively mute child to speak, Ruzicka and Sackin (1974) cited

> suggestion, persuasion, speech therapy, environmental manipulation (at times removal from the home), milieu therapy, hypnosis, behavioral modification techniques, psychoanalytic psychotherapy with or without involvement of the mother and/or father, and psychoanalysis. (p. 553)

The consistent theme in the literature is that elective mutism is difficult to treat. In fact, repeated failures have resulted from analytically oriented therapy (Kratochwill, Brody, & Piersel, 1979). While the effectiveness of behavioral therapy has been demonstrated (Kratoch-

will, et al., 1979), particularly in conjunction with family involvement, only one publication has described such an approach with family therapy (Rosenberg & Lindblad, 1978).

This family therapy approach combines ecostructural family theory with behavioral theory. The first step is to work with the family and school to assess the dysfunctional ecosystem. While working with the family and the school, behavioral principles are used because the symptom has been found so resistant to most forms of therapy. A combination of therapeutic strategies is employed, such as

- structural family therapy
- play enactment
- counterconditioning: successive approximations, reinforcement techniques, and stimulus fading within the clinic, home, and school settings

First Phase of Treatment

The goals of therapy in the first phase of treatment are

- joining
- structural diagnosis
- inquiry into the reasons that the problem should change
- redefinition of the problem
- setting of the treatment goals
- selection of treatment units with the family

Often, families of electively mute children are being pressured by the school to seek treatment and are highly suspicious of outside intervention. The therapist should assume a caring, but neutral stance with regard to the need for treatment. After getting acquainted, the therapist and the parent—without the children—should discuss the pros and cons of symptom removal. Throughout the process of joining and formulating a structural diagnosis, the therapist should avoid making the child the center of attention or pressuring the child to talk. It is crucial for the mother to feel safe and to have a voice in the interview, particularly if the father is included.

In Jerry's case, his mother's resistance to extrafamilial input was diminished and her motivation for change increased because of her desire to please her new husband. Despite this, however, Judy was initially cautious in giving a verbal history. The female therapist who conducted the individual interview and, subsequently, the family therapy was extremely empathic, gentle, and respectful toward her.

Out of respect for their newlywed status, the therapist first interviewed the couple alone. After affirming the new union, the therapist encouraged the couple to discuss their concerns and goals regarding the behavior of both the children; John and Judy agreed that they valued obedient behavior. Jerry's elective mutism was then redefined as a behavior problem, along with some other minor discipline problems that were occurring at home with both children. The therapist encouraged John and Judy to observe the children at home and to protect their family unit from any intrusions by the maternal grandfather. The strengths in their ability to communicate and support each other's parenting were underscored.

John's new role as stepfather was discussed, and it was suggested that, while Judy would continue to handle discipline, both would be actively nurturant.

Second Phase of Treatment

The goals of the second phase of treatment are

• introduction of play enactment and reinforcement techniques for successive approximation at home and in clinic sessions
• encouragement of parental expression of support and resolution of conflict
• introduction of stimulus fading within the clinic setting
• assessment of the school situation

The use of "play" as an enactment is one way of communicating with family members at a level meta to the family's rules. Since play involves participation in an "as if" world, it defuses anxiety about participation or affective expression in the real world. Just as children use play to create a bridge from their inner lives to the environment, the therapist can use this critical metaphorical technique to help the family venture safely from what is internally safe to a mastery of the external world. During play sessions at the clinic or at home, nonverbal behavior or verbalization attempts appropriate to structural goals and/or speech can be continually, positively reinforced.

Stimulus fading with regard to elective mutism is a gradual process:

1. The child is first encouraged to speak to familiar persons (i.e., the mother or siblings).

2. Less familiar persons (i.e., the father, significant relative, therapist, teacher) are then included in the setting, unobtrusively at first. Gradually, their proximity to the child is increased.

3. Less familiar persons begin asking the child questions indirectly, by way of the mother.

4. Less familiar persons begin seeking responses directly from the child in the presence of the mother.

5. Less familiar persons seek responses from the child when the mother is not present.

6. The carry-over of speech into the classroom is programmed by having the child speak to the teacher in the presence of one or two children at first, gradually phasing in the remainder of the class.

The third interview with Jerry's family began with the mother and the two children playing with toys in the room. John then entered and gave each child an M&M each time he or she approximated speech by having a puppet speak or by pretending to speak on the telephone, or by moving in any way closer to him; he was warm and caring with the children. If he wanted to say something to Jerry, he did so through the mother; if Jerry responded in any fashion, he received a piece of candy. If either child engaged in behavior that Judy found unacceptable, she had been instructed to put that child on a chair.

After about 30 minutes, the therapist entered the room, warmly greeted the parents (especially the mother), and began to talk with them.

The therapist was friendly, but unobtrusive, with the children. When Jerry hit his sister, the therapist asked the mother to whom she could express anger. She replied that she sometimes became too angry to talk at all and the definition of Jerry's elective mutism was expanded to include his similar difficulty in expressing anger. The mother then held Jerry on her lap and told him that he could have a piece of candy at home every time he could tell her when he was angry or every time he talked to John. In the next week, Jerry stopped hitting and began talking to John through his mother at home.

Following this interview, the therapist made a school visit to talk with Jerry's teacher and to observe Jerry in the classroom. The teacher was receptive to the treatment plan. Observations of Jerry revealed physical constriction and passivity with no peer interactions or speech. The teacher did not expect Jerry to talk, but she did expect him to follow her directions, which he did.

One play enactment used in the four subsequent family sessions revolved around Gardner's (1975) Talking, Feeling, and Doing game. This game was selected because of its emphasis on adhering to the rules of the game. A player selects a talking, feeling, or doing card, ranging in affective content or situations from positive affect and humorous experiences to sad, angry, or tense situations. The player receives a reward chip and a piece of candy for giving an appropriate response. While the format of this board game was considered congruent with the family's constricted style, the cards were pre-selected for content items that would elicit verbal expressions of anger, humor, and a range of nonverbal physical movement.

The mother was in charge of the rules of the game, just as she was in charge of discipline at home. Similarly, the stepfather gave nurturing rewards both in sessions and at home. Over time, these roles were varied. As the parents laughed at each other's responses, Jerry allowed himself to enter the game. After one of these sessions, he was talking directly to his stepfather in the clinic setting. Play enactment, such as drawings and puppet shows, that involved only Jerry and his stepfather further developed their relationship. In general, the family enjoyed the warmth and humor of these enactments; frequently, they lingered after the sessions.

The therapist continued to help the parents support each other, express conflict, and resolve differences, always with the stated goal of helping Jerry. Judy began to talk about how angry she became when Jerry refused to talk with John at home. They all drew pictures of the things that made them angry. Judy drew a picture of Josephine, who was talking too much, and Jerry, who was not talking with John. She told Jerry that she or John would punish him if he did not talk with John. This was the turning point in therapy, because it was the first time she had used a "loud voice" to Jerry within this enmeshed dyad. After this session, Jerry began talking directly to John at home. Contacts with the school dur-

ing this period indicated that Jerry was showing more initiative and anger.

Third Phase of Treatment

The goals of the third phase of treatment are

- resolution of conflict with others
- stimulus fading within the clinic setting, focusing on relatives, therapist, and teacher

Although the elective mute becomes progressively more familiar with the therapist with each session, direct verbal interaction with the therapist is not encouraged until the child is talking to relatives at home. Once this has been accomplished, speech is generalized to the "outside world," first the therapist, then the teacher.

The grandfather attended the eighth family session and talked with his daughter about their mutual resentments and disappointments; in this way, they developed a more positive attitude toward each other. Jerry talked directly to his grandfather during the Talking, Feeling, and Doing game and continued to do so at home.

In the ninth family session, the therapist entered the game, and speech was generalized to her. In the tenth and eleventh sessions, the kindergarten teacher was invited to be a game participant. The mother and the teacher were encouraged to chat with each other like old friends. Together with the stepfather, they pretended to be elephants and marched around the room. The mother then asked the teacher to read the cards and dispense the rewards while she left the room with the therapist. Jerry casually responded directly to the teacher as the game continued. Verbal interaction with the teacher was maintained in the next session. Consequently, the teacher began to expect Jerry to talk at school. A strong link between the mother and the teacher was encouraged, with the mother visiting the school and the teacher visiting the home.

Final Phase of Treatment

The goals of the final phase of treatment are

• stimulus fading to the school setting
• strengthening of changes within the family and child
• follow-up evaluation

In the final phase of treatment, the therapist encourages spontaneous speech with the teacher and peers at school. Modified family patterns are underscored. The child's spontaneity in physical activity and speech is expanded, particularly in regard to aggressive expression.

During the 12th and 13th sessions, the parents continued to report on the positive changes in Jerry. Not only was he asking questions of everyone easily, but he was spontaneously telling them when he was angry. His oppositional behavior had markedly decreased, and he was doing chores willingly. The parents were relating well. Play enactments used during this period were bowling and hitting Bobo the clown. The

mother made a list of what made the children angry, and each was required to express that anger verbally before being allowed to punch Bobo. The children displayed spontaneous verbalizations, humor, and a wider range of physical movement through these play enactments.

Jerry was increasing his verbal behavior with the teacher and other children in school, although it took longer to generalize his speech to the children than to the teacher. By the end of treatment, however, Jerry was reported to have become verbally angry at another child and tattled about that child to the teacher!

A follow-up 2 years later indicated that Jerry had successfully completed first grade, talked with teachers and children, and participated easily in an oral reading group.

CONCLUSION

Families with young children who elect to be mute are caught in their own theater of the absurd in which silent conversation has more import than does speech in the outside world. During family therapy, the world of play becomes a dress rehearsal for future roles; themes enacted in play prove to be the cognitive/affective experiential templates for use in the outside world. Bit parts and new voices are applauded and rewarded within the family drama by gifts that symbolically melt in the mouth. Outsiders seen as villains are transformed into clowns or fuzzy bears as they adhere to the rules of the make-believe game. As the maternal director feels empowered by her leading man and/or the audience, she creates scenarios that break the magic spell, transforming the life of the family so that they can live happily ever after.

BIBLIOGRAPHY

Bakwin, H., & Bakwin, R.M. (1972). *Behavior disorders in children*. Philadelphia: W.B. Saunders.

Bradley, W., & Sloman, L. (1975). Elective mutism in immigrant families. *Journal of the American Academy of Child Psychiatry, 14*, 510–514.

Brown, J., & Lloyd, H. (1975). A controlled study of children not speaking at school. *Journal of Associated Workers Maladjusted Children, 10*, 49–63.

Browne, E., Wilson, V., & Layborune, P. (1963). Diagnosis and treatment of elective mutism in children. *Journal of the American Academy of Child Psychiatry, 2*, 605–617.

Friedman, R., & Karagan, N. (1973). Characteristics and management of elective mutism in children. *Psychology in the Schools, 10*, 249–252.

Fundudis, T., Kolvin, I., & Garside, R. (1979). *Speech retarded and deaf children: Their psychological development*. London: Academic Press.

Gardner, R. (1975). *Psychotherapeutic approaches to the resistant child*. New York: Jason Aronson.

Goll, K. (1979). Role structure and subculture in families of elective mutists. *Family Process, 18*, 55–68.

Hayden, R. (1980). Classification of elective mutism. *Journal of the American Academy of Child Psychiatry, 19*, 118–133.

Hesselman, S. (1983). Elective mutism in children: 1877–1981. *Acta Paedopsychiatrica, 49*, 297–310.

Kolvin, I., & Fundudis, T. (1981). Elective mute children: Psychological development and background factors. *Journal of Child Pschology and Psychiatry and Allied Disciplines, 22*, 219–232.

Kratochwill, T.R., Brody, G.H., & Piersel, W.C. (1979). Elective mutism in children. In B.B. Lahey & A.E. Kazdin (Eds.), *Advances in clini-*cal child psychology (pp. 193–239). New York: Plenum Press.

Meyers, S. (1984). Elective mutism in children: A family systems approach. *American Journal of Family Therapy, 12*, 39–45.

Minuchin, S., Baker, L., Rosman, B., Liebman, R., Milman, L., & Todd, T. (1975). A conceptual model of psychosomatic illness in children. *Archives of General Psychiatry, 32*, 1031–1038.

Muller-Guggenbuhl, F. (1958). The three ravens. *Swiss-alpine folk tales*. London: Oxford University Press.

Parker, E., Olsen, T., & Throckmorton, M. (1960). Social casework with elementary school children who do not talk in school. *Social Work, 5*, 64–70.

Pustrom, E., & Speers, R. (1964). Elective mutism in children. *Journal of the American Academy of Child Psychiatry, 3*, 287–297.

Rosenberg, J., & Lindblad, M. (1978). Behavior therapy in a family context: Treating elective mutism. *Family Process, 17*, 77–82.

Ruzicka, B., & Sackin, H. (1974). Elective mutism: The impact of the patient's silent detachment upon the therapist. *Journal of the American Academy of Psychiatry, 13*, 551–561.

Tramer, M. (1934). Elektiver mutismus bei kindern. *Zeitschrift fuer Kinderpsychiatrie, 1*, 30–35.

Wergeland, H. (1979). Elective mutism. *Acta Psychiatrica Scandinavia, 59*, 218–228.

Wilkins, R. (1985). A comparison of elective mutism and emotional disorders in children. *British Journal of Psychiatry, 146*, 198–203.

Wright, H.L. (1968). A clinical study of children who refuse to talk in school. *Journal of the American Academy of Child Psychiatry, 7*, 603–617.

Youngerman, J. (1979). The syntax of silence: Electively mute therapy. *International Review of Psychoanalysis, 6*, 283–295.

5

Family Therapy for Children with Chronic Illness

Karlotta L. Bartholomew, PhD
Coordinator, Young Adult Unit
Child and Family Inpatient Service
Philadelphia Child Guidance Clinic
Philadelphia, Pennsylvania

F AMILY THERAPISTS ARE accustomed to working with families that have children with behavioral and emotional problems. They understand the developmental tasks of the family and the child, as well as the common goal of all therapeutic approaches: the development of optimal autonomy. The attainment of autonomy for children with chronic illness and their families has particular challenges for the therapist. In order to understand these challenges and develop strategies to overcome the obstacles to autonomy created by the chronic illness, the family therapist must ask not only the usual questions about the nature of the child's problem, but also three additional, crucial questions:

1. What is the nature of the illness?
2. How has the family organized around the illness?
3. Who are the people involved, and what context do they provide?

In treating chronically ill children and their families, the family therapist must be flexible. It is necessary to collaborate with various health care providers and, at times, to be a consultant in other areas, such as the family-school system. The family therapist may need to become a family-health care system-school therapist. In these roles, the therapist must find a place within the larger system, the context of the child's life.

A 14-year-old brittle diabetic boy, Chris, and his family were referred for assessment for possible psychiatric

Acknowledgments to Etienne Phipps, Anthony Rostain, and Braulio Montalvo who have influenced my thinking in this area. This chapter is dedicated to Elena Fontanari who died May 1, 1985. She taught me about living with a chronic illness.

43

inpatient care. Chris had known about his diabetes since he was 7 years of age. During the last 3 years, he had been hospitalized for ketoacidosis with increasing frequency, about once a month the last year. His hometown pediatrician had been carefully evaluating Chris' condition, seeking the organic cause of these diabetic crises. Believing that the basis of Chris' problem was indeed organic in origin, the pediatrician referred the family to Children's Hospital of Philadelphia for further evaluation. The chief of endocrinology at the hospital reviewed the previous thorough medical evaluations and current results, determined that there was a major psychosomatic component, and referred the family to the Philadelphia Child Guidance Clinic for inpatient assessment.

Initially, the parents were hesitant. They had never been told before that Chris' medical crises had a major psychosomatic component. They thought that psychiatric hospitalization was an extreme intervention. The Chief of Endocrinology was called in to meet with the parents again, as he was the only one empowered to break the parents' reluctant set and reframe the perception of the problem from organic to psychosomatic. The family's reluctance to hospitalize their son 3½ hours away from home disappeared when they were told that the situation was lethal.

At the inpatient assessment interview with the family (Chris, his mother, his father, and his 12-year-old sister, Tracey), the therapist was struck by how attractive, caring, and articulate they were. There was a great deal of friendly bantering. In talking with the family about their perception of the problem, the therapist became worried about how helpless the family felt and how powerful the "diabetes" had become. How had Chris arrived at such a potentially lethal state? How could the therapist help the family to see Chris' problem in a different way? How could the therapist go beneath the pleasant exterior to see how this family really lived together? How had the diabetes organized the family?

The Children's Hospital pediatrician who attended the session stated that she was reluctant to think of the problem only as psychosomatic and did not want anyone to forget that Chris had a disease. This was a confusing remark, but it revealed important information about her perception of Chris' problem. It would be necessary to determine how her perception of the problem affected the pattern of relationships among Chris, his family, and the therapist. The attending physician was an important player. She represented medical authority. Without her empowerment, the family therapist was helpless to confront the family to change.

THE NATURE OF THE ILLNESS

To determine the nature of the illness, the therapist must ask:

1. What are the demands in terms of medical care during the course of the illness?

2. What are the demands on the family to provide this care?

3. What is the impact of the demands of the chronic illness on the family's and child's development of autonomy?

The family therapist should begin to build a good collaborative relationship with the referring physician by asking the first two questions when accepting the referral. With the physician, the therapist needs to determine whether the reason for the referral is (1) the family's lack of knowledge about how to care for the chronically ill child, (2) a normal family response to the stressful demands of a chronic illness, (3) another problem in the family, or (4) a problem in the interaction of the family and the health care system.

While it is important for the family therapist to become familiar with the medical care demands of the illness, the therapist should not become the medical educator; that is the responsibility of the attending physician and the health care system. The therapist should concentrate on the impact of chronic illness on normal family life (see McCollum, 1981; Pray, 1983; Sargent & Baker, 1983; Travis, 1976). Although different illnesses have different effects, chronic illnesses all intrude on some aspects of family life; for example, they

- disrupt family routine
- interrupt sleep
- create physical burdens
- need complicated diets and extra housekeeping chores
- pose a financial burden
- require housing adaptation
- affect family size
- alter the structure and relationships within the family

For the child, chronic illness creates differences in socialization experiences (e.g., school) and disrupts basic childhood tasks, in particular the child's development of autonomy.

Rolland (1984) provided a psychosocial typology for categorizing similarities and differences in the effects of chronic illnesses. He chose the following four variables because of their value in assessing the relationship between the family and the individual dynamics of chronic illness over time:

1. onset (acute or gradual)
2. course (progressive, constant, or relapsing/episodic)
3. outcome (the initial expectations, the extent to which the illness is a likely cause of death, and the degree to which it can shorten life span)
4. incapacitation (impairment of cognition, sensation, movement, and energy production, as well as disfigurement)

Rolland then explored within each category the kind of stressor that each variable might present to the individual and family. The demands of an illness may vary in terms of the amount, frequency, and duration of family readjustment; the changes in roles; the problem solving required; and coping demands. Rolland saw predictability as "a kind of meta-characteristic that overlays and colors the other attributes" (p. 251). Some illnesses can be accurately typed at diagnosis as to the actual nature of their course and the rate at which changes occur.

In addition to examining the course of the chronic illness, the family therapist should consider the time phase of the illness at which therapy begins. The chronic illness time line can be divided into three major phases:

1. crisis-oriented—prediagnosis period with symptoms, diagnosis, and initial adjustment period
2. chronic—the "long haul"
3. terminal—preterminal period, death, mourning, and resolution of loss

"Each phase has its own psychosocial tasks which require significantly different strengths, attitudes, or changes from a family" (Rolland, 1984, p. 254). While in the first phase, the family must cooperate in short-term crisis reorganization. In contrast, the crucial task of the second phase is to maintain the optimal autonomy for all family members in the face of the "pull toward mutual dependency and caretaking" (Rolland, 1984, p. 255). Modes of effective functioning in one phase may be ineffective and stifling in another.

Since Chris' diabetes had been diagnosed when he was 7, his family was now in the "long haul" phase; however, the family was functioning in a crisis mode. As Chris moved into adolescence, the number of crisis hospitalizations and the number of days absent from school increased. It was getting harder for him to reenter school. Although he maintained contact with his friends, he was gradually sharing more friends and social life with his younger sister. This was a concern because, as an adolescent, he should have been moving off with his own peer group.

His mother had quit her job 2 years ago to take care of Chris as her new job. The continuing perception that strongly shaped his mother's emotional response to Chris was that *he was a dying child*. Given this perception, she did not want to place any demands on him—"How could you hurt a dying child?" In contrast, Chris' father thought that Chris could live a normal life if he had the technically correct medical treatment. Neither Chris' father nor his hometown physician could understand why Chris' diabetes had become so unpredictable. Chris and his family were very knowledgeable about the care needed for good management of his diabetes. Chris, his parents, his teachers, and his hometown pediatrician all perceived the increased frequency of diabetic crises as a problem that was organic in nature and, therefore, unpredictable and out of their control. The family was developmentally stalled, controlled by the diabetes.

FAMILY ORGANIZATION AROUND THE CHRONIC ILLNESS

On receiving the referral, the family therapist must ascertain the specific purpose of the therapy. Is it to help the family deal with the normal tasks of coping with a chronic illness? Or, is the family struggling to maintain autonomy in the presence of a chronic illness that is "out-of-control?" Generally, the family therapist is called in for the latter reason. The family has gone through the crisis stage, has reorganized to meet that crisis, but is stalled in a dysfunctional coping pattern that thwarts the family's growth and may even create a lethal situation.

Penn (1983) studied families with a chronically ill member to see how illness affected family organization over time. She found that there was a cross-generational coalition within the family. In contrast to coalitions in other families, this coalition was not denied. In fact, it looked adaptable in that it appeared to be dictated by the demands of the illness in that it was the natural supportive response to a suffering child. Furthermore, the overinvolved rescuer (protector) role was supported by the spouse. Penn further found that these patterns of interaction became bounded. She hypothesized that these "binding interactions" were the family's response to the unpredictability of the illness course and the helplessness of the family members to change it. Thus, they conceived of change as negative. Penn found that suggesting a change in the coalition pattern increased the family's resistance to therapy and, in fact, reinforced its present, albeit painful and developmentally dysfunctional, structure.

THE PLAYERS AND THE CONTEXT THAT THEY PROVIDE

In order to work with a family that has a chronically ill child, the therapist must be aware of the context of the child's life outside of the family, especially in regard to the health care system and the school. As Penn (1983) noted, families with a chronically ill member often have more permeable boundaries and are prone to coalitions with outside care-givers. Parents often allow these outside care-givers to usurp their parental roles. Like the coalitions developed within the family, these outside coalitions are not usually denied, are motivated by good

intentions, and appear to be dictated by the demands of the illness. These coalitions are also binding interactions.

Given the susceptibility of these systems to coalition, it is especially imperative that the family therapist develop a good collaborative relationship with the family physician; roles and boundaries should be clearly delineated (Sargent, 1985). The physician has medical authority, and only the physician can empower the therapist. Without the physician's empowerment, the therapist cannot challenge the family to change (Palazzoli, Boscolo, Cecchin, & Prata, 1980).

ASSESSMENT AND INTERVENTION

The family's organization around Chris' diabetes became clear during the assessment: (1) Chris was over-indulged by his mother, (2) his father had allowed himself to be pushed to the periphery of the family, and (3) his mother and father had congenially "agreed to disagree" and had permitted their 12-year-old daughter to become the communication link between the father and the rest of the family.

It was necessary to change the mother's overprotective relationship with Chris; her indulgence appeared to be keeping him immature and may have been contributing to his present lethal medical state. Her overprotectiveness had increased over the last 2 years as Chris' medical condition had deteriorated.

The therapist's major intervention during the 2-hour assessment interview was to support the father in challenging the mother to join him in expecting Chris to grow up and be responsible for the management of his diabetes. It was necessary simultaneously to block the father from withdrawing when the mother resisted him. Finally, the mother, in tears, embraced the father. As a newly formed team, the parents set two goals for Chris during his inpatient treatment: (1) to learn diabetic self-management and (2) to learn to settle daily conflicts without turning to his parents for protection. This was temporary, but it was the first step in breaking the indulgent pattern (Bartholomew & Montalvo, 1985).

The attending pediatrician developed and coordinated the diabetic program with Chris and the inpatient staff; she saw Chris several times each week. Chris, who was very knowledgeable, managed his diabetes well during the first week; he soon started to complain and refused to follow the program, however, expressing anger at the disease. The nursing staff asked the therapist whom they should call to deal with the problem: (1) Should the inpatient treatment team set up behavioral consequences? (2) Should the parents be asked to set limits? (3) Should the attending pediatrician be called in to confront Chris?

The therapist asked the nurse to call the pediatrician, who believed that the therapist had been too challenging initially to the family, especially to Chris and his mother. She had been taught in her training that a family needs support, education, and/or new technology in coping with a chronic illness. This problem-solving paradigm differed from that of the therapist, however. Furthermore, the pediatrician had been drawn into the protective relationship with "angelic" Chris from which his mother had been temporarily removed in the assessment interview.

The intervention was successful. The pediatrician saw that "angelic" Chris was defying *her* orders. She became angry at his blatant refusal to cooperate after she had spent hours trying to be supportive and to accommodate him in developing his diabetic protocol. She marked this as the turning point in her allegiance to the family therapist and the treatment team. She had never before seen parental conflict in such congenial people exacerbate a severe medical problem in a child as it had with Chris. Thus, at this point, she began to see how an overprotective relationship with Chris kept him in his lethal medical state, and she now held Chris and his mother accountable. She empowered the family therapist, establishing the framework for the major family treatment intervention in the third week of hospitalization. At this time, from an empowered position, the therapist induced a crisis in order to dislocate the mother further from her entrenched, lethal, overprotective relationship with Chris by having the now active father push the mother to make a *clear,* unambiguous break with Chris and form a more stable alliance with him.

Several months later, the mother described that session as the most difficult hour and a half of her life. She knew that she was not with her husband—she was protecting Chris. She had believed that he was going to die, and she wanted to make the remainder of his life as pleasant as possible. She had not realized that he could grow up and be a healthy child. Her husband was relentlessly persistent, however. He insisted that she tell Chris about all her pent-up anger. He screamed at her, "You've got to do this. I don't want to bury my son in the ground. I want him alive. You have to be with me. You have to help." Finally, through sobs and tears, she yelled at Chris.

This was a turning point for the family. During the last 2 weeks of psychiatric hospitalization, Chris managed his diabetes and his conflicts with peers and staff. When he returned home, however, he tested the mettle of the new relationship between his parents and was hospitalized seven times during the first 4 months of outpatient therapy. Since the parents stabilized their working relationship, however, there has been only one hospitalization, and Chris has missed only 3 days of school in the last 2 years.

The parents had to break the pattern of overprotection in all the major institutions that were involved with Chris in their hometown. The hometown pediatrician continued to see Chris' problem as organic; however, he also respected the medical authority of the attending physician, who agreed to continue as the therapist's medical consultant until the medical conflicts about Chris' responsibility for self-management

were resolved and the hometown physician empowered the family therapist.

During the first year of outpatient therapy, Chris' mother finally learned how to hold her ground with the hometown pediatrician. She and her husband had been caught between holding Chris accountable for the management of his diabetes and risking another medical crisis. If they stepped in, however, they risked reactivating the overprotective relationship in which Chris depended on them for tasks that should be his responsibility.

In the past, Chris' mother had telephoned the pediatrician almost every day. Now she was disengaging. After one serious medical crisis, the pediatrician, very shaken, admonished the mother that they could not allow a crisis like that to occur again. Not wanting to return to living from shot to shot, the mother held her ground with the physician. In the past, she would have complied, because she and the pediatrician had each supported the other's overprotective relationship with Chris and because the physician was the medical expert. Now, well aware of the need for increased autonomy for both Chris and the family, she negotiated a mid-range plan—between hovering and disengagement—for having Chris' medical status evaluated at a local hospital instead of at home, where she and her husband would have to oversee the diabetic management. In addition, when Chris was hospitalized, she did not give him the "cuddling" that she had given him previously. Although she could not influence the hospital staff to change in that respect, she and her husband did expect Chris to test himself and keep records while he was in the hospital—much to the dismay of the hospital staff. Soon, Chris' hospital stays were shorter; he and the pediatrician worked out a management plan that required direct contact between the two of them, rather than between the mother and the physician. (Recently, the pediatrician informed Chris' mother that he now has a therapist on his staff to work with families.)

Interestingly enough, Chris' mother was in a position in her family of origin that was not dissimilar to her position in her nuclear family. She was involved in an overprotective relationship with her father, who was an out-of-control diabetic. When she broke with Chris, she also became less involved with her own mother and father. She was not conforming to her parents' expectations in regard to Chris' treatment, and she was never able to make them understand her new approach. Although things often fell apart between her parents after that, she no longer tried to hold them together. She had given up the role of protector with them, as well as with Chris.

The school continued to treat Chris as a "sick" child. The parents had created and perpetuated such an image over a 4-year period, and they now realized that they needed to change this image. They insisted that Chris return to school full-time. To their surprise, they found at the end of that year that the school had given Chris a medical absence from physical education. Although they had talked to the teachers and school nurse about holding Chris accountable for doing his schoolwork and managing his diabetes, they found that the teachers had continued to excuse him and that he had spent many hours in the nurse's office talking with her.

Together, the parents met with the principal. As a strong team, they told the principal the new plan that had to be followed. They had realized that the teachers would not change unless the principal gave them the authority and assured them that the previously "sick" Chris was able to handle both his schoolwork and his diabetes. The shift in perception was difficult for the first year. Initially, the teachers believed that the parents were being too demanding and insensitive. The situation has evolved, however; Chris is now making plans for future professional training.

CONCLUSION

Therapists must recognize that, in providing family therapy for families that have a chronically ill child, they are entering the world of the medical system. They must be empowered by medical authority as well as collaborate with the medical system.

These families are prone to develop coalitions of benign intent both within and without the family, especially at developmental points of marked change. As Chris' father said a year and a half after inpatient treatment, "The biggest difference is that our family no longer has diabetes. Chris has it, and we are no longer his conscience."

It is a constant struggle for these families and for their individual members to maintain and develop autonomy, not only because of the physical, emotional, and economic demands and effects of the illness, but also because of the frequent intrusions of other systems (e.g., medical, educational) into their lives. A major task of the family therapist is to assist these families in maintaining their autonomy, their own sense of competence, and their sense of hope.

REFERENCES

Bartholomew, K., & Montalvo, B. (1985). *You go where you get it: Assessment of a brittle diabetic boy and his family* [Videotape]. Philadelphia: Philadelphia Child Guidance Clinic.

Hochman, G. (1984). Anatomy of a recovery. *American Health, 3*(7), 74–78.

McCollum, A. (1981). *The chronically ill child: A guide for parents and professionals.* New Haven, CT: Yale University Press.

Palazzoli, M., Boscolo, L., Cecchin, G., & Prata, G. (1980). The problem of the referring person. *Journal of Marriage and Family Therapy, 6,* 3–9.

Penn, P. (1983). Coalition and binding interactions in families with chronic illness. *Family Systems Medicine, 1*(2), 16–25.

Pray, L. (1983). *Journey of a diabetic.* New York: Simon & Schuster.

Rolland, J. (1984). Toward a typology of chronic and life-threatening illness. *Family Systems Medicine, 2*(3), 245–262.

Sargent, J. (1985). Physician-family therapist collaboration: Children with medical problems. *Family Systems Medicine, 3*(4), 454–465.

Sargent, J., & Baker, L. (1983). Behavior and diabetes care. *Primary Care, 10,* 583–594.

Travis, G. (1976). *Chronic illness in children: Its impact on child and family.* Stanford, CA: Stanford University Press.

6

Sibling Therapy with Children in Foster Homes

Karen Gail Lewis, ACSW
Eating Disorders Clinic
University of Cincinnati
Cincinnati, Ohio

S IBLING THERAPY IS A STYLE of providing family therapy systematically, even when the family is fragmented. When the separated siblings are seen together, their behavior may improve, and their sense of family may increase. If they are feeling a stronger sense of family (even if only through their sibling connection), their adjustment in a foster home may be smoother. The method described here focuses on siblings not living in the same foster home, but it is equally applicable to those living together. (Elsewhere, I have written about treatment goals for children from multi-problem families, the role of fighting in their communication, and treatment themes and interventions in working with these children (Lewis, 1983, 1984, in press).) Here I will identify some problems for the foster children and their foster parents, and I will describe sibling therapy, focusing on the role of the therapist and the integration of the presenting problem with the development of the sibling bond (Bank & Kahn, 1982).

DIFFICULTIES IN DEFINING THE DIFFICULT FAMILY

Although there are many definitions of the difficult family, the most accurate one is rarely used: a difficult family is one with whom the therapist is having difficulty. This article will address one type of difficulty—the family fragmented by foster home placements certainly qualifies as a difficult family. One of the factors that makes such a family "difficult" is the complexity of identifying who should be included in the family. This complicated problem has been considered from the viewpoint of remarriage (Visher & Visher, 1982), but it is an equally complicated question when the Department of Social Services (DSS), not the parents, has custody of the children. To make matters even more complex, siblings in the custody of DSS are often living in several different foster homes. Therefore, siblings referred to community mental health centers by the DSS may be in different catchment areas, and it is not uncommon for more than one DSS worker to be involved. It is also not uncommon for DSS workers dealing with siblings to be unaware of or to have no contact with each other and the other siblings.

A DSS worker referred Karry, aged 8, to the local mental health center for individual therapy. Karry has been in foster care for approximately 8 months. Her mother was alcoholic, and her father was abusive. Karry adjusted very well for the first few weeks in the foster home; in the week before the referral, however, she had defecated in the dresser drawer and set fire to the toilet paper. The DSS worker required an immediate interview for Karry.

Another DSS worker had called the previous week about Billy, aged 4, who had tried to jump out of a second-story window. The intake therapist had no way of knowing that Billy, who was also in a foster home, was Karry's younger brother. The DSS worker who brought Karry to the first appointment also brought Darleen, aged 7, Karry's younger sister; Darlene lived in yet another foster home. The DSS worker was requesting that Darlene be seen by still another therapist because of her underachievement at school. As it turned out, Karry was one of seven children who were living in six different foster homes and being followed by three different DSS workers. Two of the brothers were already in individual therapy in a different community mental health center.

The intake worker trying to choose a treatment plan for Karry may believe that her problem stems from her early deprivation, from visitation problems with her natural parents, or from problems within the foster home. All of these explanations are possible, but there are many other possible explanations. None of these factors alone represents the whole picture.

Where, then, should the therapist start? With the foster parents? With the natural parents, who are already in individual therapy, marital therapy, and alcohol counseling? Should the four therapists involved with the natural parents be seen? Should their supervisors be included? How about the three DSS workers and their supervisors? What about the therapists for all the siblings and their supervisors? Should the consultants, parents of the natural parents and parents of the foster parents, and all the children living with each foster family be included as well? Family therapists at community mental health centers are faced with a real dilemma. They are trained to see the whole family and to think systemically. In this situation, however, who is the family? Even if the therapist believes that everyone is part of the problem (Imber-Black (Coppersmith), 1984), it may be impossible to gather everyone together and reach an agreement on the best treatment plan. Even when the agency therapist looks to the larger system, frequently siblings are not considered in the planning.

PROBLEMS OF FOSTER CHILDREN

Many problems are specific to children in foster homes. The two that are germane, here, are related to the transition from the natural family to the foster family and include separation from the natural family and continued loyalty and attachment to them.

Foster children may not be able to rely on their natural parents' consistent presence and nurturing; however, their siblings may provide a stabilizing influence. Courts sometimes proscribe parental contact with children, but they rarely curtail sibling visitation. Conversely, courts may arrange for parental visitation, but they rarely specify visits for siblings. For children without adequate parenting, the sibling contact becomes even more significant. Lack of consistent parenting can be devastating to a child, yet a strong sibling bond can be a more than adequate substitute.

Bank and Kahn (1982) note that strong bonds can develop among siblings who have a need for meaningful personal identity, have had insufficient parental influence, and have high access to each other. Access is high when siblings are close in age and share friends, clothes, and life experiences; therefore, high access children are likely to have a significant influence on each other's personality and feelings. However, even when children from multi-problem families have high access to each other, the problems may become disruptive to their relationship (Bank & Kahn, 1982).

If the children were close before their separation, they may have a foundation for maintaining the relationship. Unfortunately, many of the foster children seen in treatment have been separated repeatedly from their siblings, preventing the development of this kind of attachment. While there is no automatic instinct for sibling connection, therapists may try to develop the sense of family. The siblings may not be a consistent presence in the youngsters' lives, but the therapist may be able to create a sense of lasting relationships that transcends some of the transience of their situations.

Regardless of their family relationships, children maintain a loyalty to their natural families. This is demonstrated by the difficulties that many children have in foster homes that are considerably more loving and nurturing than their own homes are. Problems that arise in therapy and in foster homes are often related to this loyalty conflict. Therapists must be careful not to offer more affection than the children can accept without feeling disloyal. Similarly, foster parents must understand that some of these children's misbehavior may be related to this loyalty conflict. In fact, the warmer and more caring the foster family, the greater the conflict may be.

PROBLEMS OF FOSTER PARENTS

Foster parents are often seen as resistant to participating in the foster child's therapy. It is more likely that they already feel overburdened without the extra effort of attending the foster child's therapy. As one foster mother put it, "I have about 35 foster children a year. If I had to go to all their therapies, I would be doing nothing else but that." This is not resistance; this is reality.

Foster parents have their own problems. They frequently have children from different families, often with siblings placed elsewhere. They may have no information about the foster child, the natural parents, the siblings, or the child's home situation. The children that they take in often have serious emotional problems. Foster parents may have had only limited training to help them understand family systems (Katz & Sherman, 1985*) or deal with the specific problems of the child. Furthermore, many foster parents are raising their own children and have their own family, marital, or financial problems. Sometimes they themselves are in therapy.

Therapists can be of help to foster parents even without meeting them directly. Periodic telephone calls not only keep the foster parents informed of treatment issues and progress, but also allow the therapist to help the foster parents handle specific behavior problems.

When Karry set the toilet paper on fire, the therapist was able to inform the foster mother that Karry's home had burned down the week before. Her natural parents and her 2-month-old baby brother, the only ones in the home at the time of the fire, had all been moved somewhere else; however, Karry did not know where they were. The evening after this telephone call, the foster mother talked with Karry about her parents and baby brother. She said that she cared about Karry, but would never try to replace Karry's own mother. She also offered to help Karry contact the DSS worker the next morning to find out where her parents were living. The problems with defecating and setting fires never recurred. Because of her conversation with the therapist, the foster mother understood Karry's feelings and was able to help Karry express her anxiety verbally. This eliminated her need to express it behaviorally.

SIBLING THERAPY

The therapist's dilemma is how best to help the individual child who has a specific problem. Family therapists believe that involving the family system is the best way to help troubled children. When the larger system or any of the smaller subsystems are unavailable, the therapist must use whatever contextual resources remain. It is often difficult to determine which context—the natural family, the foster family, or the mental health professionals—offers the most useful resources, however, and to get the people involved in the child's ecosystem to participate in treatment. Sibling therapy focuses on one subsystem, the siblings, with the general goal of increasing its awareness of itself as a related system

---

*Katz, A., & Sherman, C. (1985). Personal communication about a training program they are running at the Children's Center in Hamden, CT, entitled "Introducing family systems concepts to foster parents for facilitating their liaison with biologic parents."

and the specific goal of eliminating the presenting problem.

Siblings automatically form a subgroup of a family. There is often a cohesiveness among them, especially when their parents are not present. Even in intact families, children spend more of their time with their siblings than with their parents. Siblings provide identification models and standards for normal behavior; they get from and give to each other approval, guidance, control, and direction. When the parents are not emotionally available, siblings can provide nurturing or "anchoring" (Minuchin, Montalvo, Guerney, Rosman, & Schumer, 1967). This has long been observed in large families (Bossard & Boll, 1956) in which the older children have cared for the younger ones. In disrupted families, then, siblings can become their own family network. Sibling therapy makes it possible to develop this sibling network.

Involving the siblings in treatment can have immediate benefits. The identified patient gets symptom relief, and the siblings see each other. There are also long-term benefits. It is likely that the families of children in foster care have been in turmoil for many years. The children are likely to be having problems in school, in the foster home, and in their relationships with peers. There may be no consistent parenting, but sibling therapy can at least provide consistent family contact through the siblings. Brothers and sisters in these situations are bound together not only through blood, but also through the common bond of shared family crises. Some children from multiproblem families automatically pull together for support, but others have experienced so many physical and emotional separations that they have never had the opportunity to develop a relationship with any of the other siblings. This is especially true for children who have been placed in different foster homes.

The logistics of sibling therapy can become very complicated. It is often difficult to coordinate schedules and transportation for children living in different parts of town. When foster parents do not bring the children to therapy, the DSS workers must do so. This is a time-consuming task for them, but many DSS workers are relieved to have one therapist helping all the siblings with their emotional problems.

Integration of Specific Goals with Relationship Goals

Family therapists have long understood that, when one member of a family has a problem, all members of that family have a problem. In some ways, this is even truer for children from multi-problem families. If one child has a problem so severe that it interferes with the child's ability to rely on the other siblings, it becomes a severe problem for all the siblings. The removal of any one possible source of connection or nurturance further decreases the already limited emotional resources of these families. If the therapist teaches the siblings to notice each other, to be empathic toward each other, and to care what happens to each other, the children may learn to rely on each other for emotional nurturance. In contrast to the DSS worker, the foster parents, and the school staff, who may be interested simply in symptom removal, the therapist attends to these relationship issues in addition to the symptom.

Role of the Therapist

While there is much that therapists can do to help these children, input needs to be limited to what is feasible given the world in which they live. Children may see a therapist once a week, at best; they spend the other 10,020 minutes of the week in a world that may not offer them as much understanding. Therefore, the therapist needs to set modest treatment goals that are specific and directed both at resolving the immediate problem and at supporting the relationships within the sibling subsystem (Lewis, in press).

There is a natural evolution in sibling therapy that limits the role of the therapist. Although the therapist begins as a central person in the session, the therapist becomes less involved as the relationships develop between the siblings and they become more available to each other without the therapist as intermediary. These children need a caring, consistent person in their lives; the natural parents, the frequently changing foster parents, and the DSS workers are

often unable to play this role. It is hoped that it will not have to be the therapist, either. The therapist's objective during the sessions is to decrease his or her own importance and increase the children's interdependence.

The following diagrams, based on Andolfi's dismantling of a rigid family system (Andolfi, Angelo, Menghi, & Nicolo-Corigliano, 1983), show the evolving and then diminishing role of the therapist and the building of cohesion among the siblings taking place in various stages:

1. Stage One (Figure 1). The first session is often chaotic. This is the first time that many of these siblings have been together in the same room for any length of time. The level of anxiety, which is high, is matched by the levels of noise and activity. The children enter the room without knowing the therapist.

2. Stage Two (Figure 2). In the second stage, which starts immediately, the therapist becomes the central figure, organizing the activity, intervening in conflicts, and dealing with each child directly. This is the most common role for group therapists who work with children (Garland, Jones, & Kolodny, 1965).

3. Stage Three (Figure 3). While remaining in the center, the therapist helps the children relate to each other by bringing two siblings together around a specific game or activity, or by directing two siblings to have a specific discussion. For example, "John, ask Bill if he wants to play with you." "Carol is playing with dolls, too. Why don't you go sit near her, Lily?" "I need some help string-

Figure 1 The Therapist as an Invisible Member of the Group

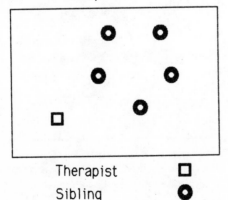

Therapist   □

Sibling   ●

Figure 2 The Therapist as the Central Member of the Group

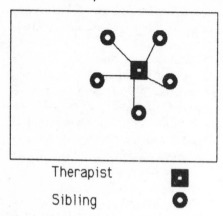

Therapist ▪

Sibling ○

ing these beads. Lenny and Laura, will you help me?''

4. Stage Four (Figure 4). The siblings relate more to each other, and the therapist moves out of the center. If a leader is needed, the parental child becomes central, with the therapist available as a coach. For many families, treatment may not last long enough to reach this stage.
5. Stage Five (Figure 5). In the ideal post-therapy relationship, the therapist is no longer needed; the siblings can support, nurture, and assist each other. This stage may never be reached while the siblings are young children, but it is a model of what they can achieve as they grow older.

Understanding the stages of the group's development is one of the therapist's roles. A second important role is orchestrating the multiple agenda. The therapist has a difficult balancing act in developing the sibling relationship while addressing the immediate problem and providing activities that keep the children interested and involved. Ideally, the therapist uses both the discussion of the immediate problem and the action within the room to cement the sibling relationships.

CASE EXAMPLE

In the following case example, the therapist used a group activity to develop the relationship among the siblings in order to help Suzi with her withdrawn and suicidal behavior. The therapist was working as a matchmaker (i.e., Stage Three).

Suzi, aged 5, was the youngest of four children. Meg, aged 12, was in one foster home; Kenny, aged 10, and Petey, aged 7, were in another; and Suzi was in a third. Suzi had been placed separately because of her withdrawn and suicidal behavior. Suzi stared into space or talked to herself most of the day. She seemed unaware of the presence of others. The week before her referral for therapy, she had tried to cut herself with a

Figure 3 The Therapist as a Matchmaker

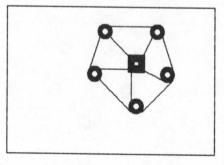

Therapist ▪

Sibling ○

Figure 4 The Therapist as a Coach

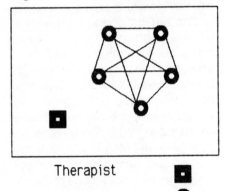

Therapist ▪

Sibling ◉

knife, and her foster parents wanted her to be hospitalized. The DSS worker had requested therapy for her until a hospital bed was available. The other three children were all doing poorly in school. Kenny was constantly fighting with schoolmates, Petey was shy and withdrawn, and Meg was bossy and disliked.

The children paid no attention to each other as they entered the therapy room, even though it had been several weeks since they had seen each other. They ran around the room grabbing whatever toy they could reach, fiddling with it for a few minutes, and then moving on to something else. After giving the children some time to explore the room and the toys, the therapist engaged the three older children in a game of tag. It was a physical activity that required neither skill nor prolonged attention. It allowed them to move and scream, and any motion away from the game could be reframed as part of the game. Although Suzi was invited to join the game, she stared into space or colored.

While the children were playing tag, the therapist talked to them about Suzi. Did they know why she stared into space or stayed by herself? Did they know about the knife? Why would she have wanted to kill herself? Did anyone know whether Suzi might be feeling lonely? These and other questions were filtered through the noise of the game and were virtually ignored. The therapist mused aloud about some possibilities. Periodically, the therapist whispered to the child who was "It" to go tag Suzi. Although Suzi herself appeared not to notice these contacts, the other three children were at least being made aware of her presence.

Over snacks, the therapist guided the discussion. How did they think Suzi was feeling about going to the hospital? How would they feel if they were not allowed to see her? How might she feel if they were not allowed to see her? How did they think she might feel living in a foster home without a brother or sister? This

Figure 5 The Therapist as a Former Therapist

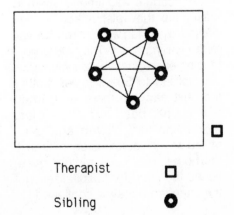

Therapist ☐

Sibling ◉

time, sitting quietly to eating and having heard the questions before, the three older siblings responded. Their comments were surprisingly insightful. Petey asked Suzi if she wanted half of one of his cookies; she looked at him and smiled. Not to be outdone, Kenny went over and hugged Suzi, telling her that he did not want her to kill herself. Meg was most able to talk about the feelings of being alone and scared. With prompting from the therapist, she told Suzi how she would feel when Suzi went to the hospital. She said that she bet Suzi would feel as lonely and as scared as she herself did at night when all the adults went to bed and she was alone in the bedroom.

Suzi did not say anything in response to her brothers and sister, but she looked very carefully at each of them. Then, without any warning, she got up and began running around the room. At first, she appared quite psychotic. Then the therapist realized that Suzi was tagging her brothers and sister as she ran. She was imitating the game of tag that they had been playing earlier. Although it was time for them to leave, the therapist asked if they wanted to play tag with Suzi on the way to the waiting room. They all ran out tagging each other—Suzi included!

In talking to Suzi's foster mother the next day, the therapist learned that Suzi had been very different that night. She had played and even talked with the other foster children in the home. The foster mother questioned the need for hospitalization if the changed behavior continued.

Three months later, the children were all moved to new foster homes in another catchment area. They were assigned to four different therapists for individual therapy. A telephone call to one of the new DSS workers revealed that Suzi had not been hospitalized. Although she was still withdrawn, she played with other children and had made no other suicide gestures. Meg called Suzi periodically and was trying to arrange a sibling get-together for one of the holidays.

SUMMARY

Family therapy with young children can be chaotic and difficult. When there is no family or many families, as is the case with children in foster homes, it becomes even more difficult. The challenge for the therapist is to find a way of working with the identified child as well as attending to the systemic issues around the child. Addressing the entire system may be overwhelming or not feasible. Sibling therapy provides a means of intervening with the presenting problem for the identified child while also assisting with the sibling relationships and problems of daily life. Telephone contacts and periodic meetings with foster and natural parents, all involved DSS workers, and other agency professionals can further underscore the systemic effects of the interventions. Given the inevitable problems and chaos of the court system, the DSS system, and the CMHC, sibling therapy may provide a thread of consistency and predictability for these youngsters which not only helps with the immediate problems of adjustment but builds a trust bank for future relationships.

REFERENCES

Andolfi, M., Angelo, C., Menghi, P., & Nicolo-Corigliano, M. (1983). *Behind the family mask: Therapeutic change in rigid family systems.* New York: Brunner/Mazel.

Bank, S., & Kahn, M. (1982). *Sibling bond.* New York: Basic Books.

Bosaard, J.H.S., & Boll, E.S. (1956). *The large family system.* Philadelphia: University of Pennsylvania Press.

Garland, J., Jones, H., & Kolodny, R. (1965). A model for stages of development in social work groups. In S. Bernstein (Ed.), *Explorations in group work: Essays in theory and practice.* Boston: Boston University School of Social Work.

Imber-Black (Coppersmith), E. (1984). The systemic consultant and human service provider systems. In L. Wynne (Ed.), *Family therapist as consultant.* New York: Guilford Press.

Lewis, K.G. (1983). Sibling therapy. *Family Therapy News, 14,* 12. Washington, DC: Association for Marriage and Family Therapy.

Lewis, K.G. (1984). Sibling therapy, Part II. *Family Therapy News, 15,* 7. Washington, DC: Association for Marriage and Family Therapy.

Lewis, K.G. (in press). Sibling therapy with multiproblem families. *Journal of Marital and Family Therapy.*

Minuchin, S., Montalvo, B., Guerney, B.G., Jr., Rosman, B.L., & Schumer, F. (1967). *Families of the slums: An exploration of their structure and treatment.* New York: Basic Books.

7

Families with Young Disabled Children in Family Therapy

Martha A. Foster, PhD
Associate Professor
Department of Psychology
Georgia State University

ALTHOUGH FAMILIES WITH A disabled child share with all families the predictable dilemmas of family life and child-rearing, three features distinguish them. First, a developmental disability is usually a lifelong, chronic condition that limits a child's functioning and requires the family to deal with its core values. The family is challenged to make some kind of sense out of the fact that one of its members will have fewer life options than others have and to recognize the fact that a significant portion of the disabled member's identity will be associated with the disability. Second, it is often a more complicated task for parents of disabled children than for other parents to maintain the always delicate balance between protecting and challenging children. Patterns of overprotection are common in the parents of disabled children. Third, families with a disabled child are required to deal with a greater number of service systems and helping professionals than are other families during the course of child-rearing. The risk of triangles and miscommunications is particularly high.

Disabled children also face special challenges. Most disabled children must struggle to forge an identity that accommodates in a positive way the stigma of their disability. In addition, their relationship with their parents, the primary context in which they develop a functional balance between dependence and autonomy, is frequently hampered by their own anxieties and limitations, as well as by those of their parents. Furthermore, the host of helping professionals and agencies with whom many deal is often a significant reference group that has both positive and negative effects on their social development. Although family therapy for families with a disabled child proceeds as it does with any family that has a child-centered problem, the family therapist who is sensitive to the disabled child's perspective has a more complete picture of the system and, if willing to engage with the child, an alternate path toward change.

THE LABEL OF DISABILITY

Despite educational, medical, and therapeutic programs, most disabled children face restricted options in their social relationships, in school achievement, and in the degree of independent living possible. While most visible at the time of diagnosis, parents' sorrow about their child's disability is recurrent and often resurfaces at life cycle transitions that underline the differences between their child and other children. Marker events, such as the first day of school, religious rituals, or graduation, can evoke painful feelings thought to have been overcome long ago. Therapists working with families with a disabled child must be sensitive to these normal, predictable feelings and must not assume that they are part of a pathological grief process.

Parents may also be concerned about the potential long-term effects of the disabled child on their nondisabled children.

After the birth of a baby with Down's syndrome, the mother's anxieties became riveted on her other child, Polly, a competent 9-year-old. The mother worried that Polly would be handicapped for life by the burden of her mentally retarded sister. Polly was displaying some signs of anxiety, which fueled the mother's assumption that the child could not cope with her new sister's condition. The few sessions of therapy focused on issues of immediate management, such as getting services for the new baby and extra household help. Because Polly's anxiety mirrored that of her parents and resulted, in part, from the disruption in family life, the therapist encouraged the mother and father to resume their prior routines with Polly. At a meeting several years later, the mother told the therapist that all were doing well in the family and she confided that she and her husband had remembered and been guided by the words, "Let's begin by getting Polly through fourth grade."

Many disabled children need help in accepting and verbalizing their distress at their inability to achieve certain skills and at their being different from their peers. Mastery of school skills and peer relationships are of paramount importance to a child's self-esteem. Just as the parents need to feel that it is all right to feel sorry for themselves sometimes, the disabled child needs validation of his or her distress. Although parents usually provide this for the child, the disabled child's feelings may also be an important therapeutic focus. Parents who have worked hard to come to terms with their own feelings about their child's disability and to obtain normal opportunities for their child may be ill-prepared to deal with depression in the child. Sensing the delicate balance that the parents have achieved, the child may protect them by masking his or her difficulty.

The Waverlys had three children; their middle child, 11-year-old Jill, had cerebral palsy and used a wheelchair. Because of the availability of on-site physical, speech, and occupational therapy, she had been attending a self-contained class for physically disabled children far from her own home. As her need for these services lessened, her parents had decided to enroll her in the nearby public school that her siblings attended. The change had entailed several school conferences, new evaluations, and considerable persistence and advocacy on the part of her parents. The family, veterans of special education politics, had discussed the move with Jill, who was enthusiastic about the change. The first term in fifth grade had gone smoothly, but Jill's outgoing personality had begun to fade by January. She developed several minor somatic symptoms, cried easily, and was irritable at home. Her consistent response to questions about school was that everything was fine, "she loved it." Her parents interpreted her behaviors as the early onset of "adolescence." When her grades began to drop, however, they sought therapy.

A school observation suggested another explanation for the problem. Although Jill was "mainstreamed" with nondisabled peers, she was often by herself during the school day. All the children spoke to her, but she did not have a group of special friends. Her teachers had noticed her loneliness, but were not sure how to help her "crack" the well-established peer groups. In an individual session with Jill, the therapist gently inquired about her isolation at school. Her initial bravado was gradually overcome until, crying, she confided that she no longer received the attention that she had received when school began; she confessed that she missed the sense of protection and easy camaraderie of friends from her old school. She felt that to share her feelings was to be disloyal to her parents, because they had such high expectations about the school change. "They worked so hard to get me in; I can't tell them I hate it and want to go back." Her peer experiences had also elicited negative feelings about her disability that she did not know how to handle.

The therapist insisted that Jill share her concerns about school with her parents, but agreed to help her talk about her problems in such a way that they would listen to her. The stage for this was set by amplifying the topic that was being discussed as the family entered the next session; Jill's older sister had recently learned that she had not been accepted at the college of her choice. By allowing a nurturing interchange between the mother and the older daughter to continue and by blocking the father's positive platitudes, the therapist established the context for disclosing negative feelings. (As is often the case, I had been clear before this session about the goal, but the specific tactic of using the sibling's recent experience as the spring board was not planned.) In therapy, the family's powerful belief in positive thinking and goal-oriented behavior, a belief system that had encouraged risk taking and achievement in everyone, was challenged just enough for Jill to share her fears and be supported.

After complimenting *both* parents for being supportive and nurturing ("It's easy to be with your kids when they're winning, but only great parents know how to hear and be helpful with the painful stuff."), the therapist asked whether all the children knew about this side of their parents' nature. They commented that their oldest child had always been more willing to tell them her problems than the two younger ones were. Aware of the father's difficulty with "feeling talk," the therapist encouraged the mother to find out if anything was bothering Jill. Several moves (e.g., rearranging seating, blocking interference by the younger brother and the father, supporting Jill's hesitant verbalizations, and tolerating many pauses) were necessary before Jill and her mother were talking. As the intensity built, the mother felt empowered to block interruptions, including those from the father. After the problem was revealed and Jill's distress validated, first by the mother and then by the others, the therapist directed them toward problem resolution, again supporting the competence of *both* parents.

Several solutions were proposed and, over several sessions, carried out by the family. Both parents encouraged Jill to resume some contact with her old friends. Her sister agreed to help her with clothes and coach her on some "teen-aged" interests that still bewildered Jill. Her parents explained the problem to her teachers; several weeks later, one teacher introduced a novel about a disabled child that sparked discussion in the class and broke down some barriers for Jill. The key to the change seemed to be a family in which they all acknowledged their feelings about Jill's disability and their sense of pressure to overachieve. For Jill, who had felt isolated with her problems at school and negative feelings about her disability, hearing her sister say "Sometimes I just want to throw that wheelchair over a cliff so I won't ever see it again!" was strangely validating.

Because of its lifelong nature, a disability must be acknowledged as "real." The most positive reframing cannot eliminate the fact of blindness or cerebral palsy in a child. Many parents struggle to find the best language to describe their child's disability. When the diagnosis is unclear or the disabilities are multiple, the therapist may help the family select the words or labels that they will use to describe their child's disability to others. Siblings, grandparents, and other relatives may participate in this process, enactment in therapy of the confusion often felt privately. The goal is to select words that are comfortable for the family, not necessarily words that the professionals would use. For example, many families refer to their mentally retarded child as "delayed" or "slow," but interact with the child in ways that indicate a clear understanding of the child's cognitive limitations. Although professionals have long interpreted parents' avoidance of some labels as denial, what matters most is the appropriateness of the parents' interactions with the child.

Families must help children with disabilities acquire words to describe their disability to others and to themselves. This should begin when the child is very young.

In a preschool classroom, the teacher was working with a small group of children who were sitting in chairs around her. As part of the routine ending of the activity, the teacher called each child's name, saying "OK, _____, you may go to the art table." One 3-year-old girl in long leg braces watched each child stand up in turn. Finally, she looked down at her own legs and seemed to study them; then, with a puzzled expression, she looked up at the teacher as if to say "Why can't I?" At that moment, one of those "teachable moments," the teacher explained to the child that she had spina bifida, that her legs did not work right, but that she, too, could walk with the help of her braces and walker. Shortly thereafter, in a session with her parents, the therapist explored ways to explain the disability to the child and what words they would help her use to describe her disability to others.

For school-aged children, particularly those with visible disabilities, the ability to explain their condition and adaptive equipment (e.g., wheelchairs, braces) to peers can be a social asset. Because it is considered impolite to mention another's limitation in our culture, disabled persons must usually explain their condition in order to alleviate the discomfort of those around them who are aware of it, but feel restricted from comment.

Children with less visible handicaps, such as learning disabilities, may need particular help in understanding their problems. Often, they have a history of academic failure or sanctions for behavioral problems that has eroded their self-confidence and self-esteem. The therapist may use drawings, puppets, or therapeutic techniques like mutual story-telling (Gardner, 1971), and puppets to discern the way in which these children perceive themselves. Many fear that they are mentally retarded or just "stupid;" others worry about being "crazy." Sometimes, a child's confusion mirrors confusion at the parental level about the nature or severity of the disability; resolution of the parental confusion permits resolution of the child's confusion.

PARENT-CHILD RELATIONSHIPS

Parenting comprises a continuing series of situations in which parents must decide whether to push or protect their children, whether to hold on to them or let them go. Some decisions are clear, such as allowing a child to risk some tumbles in order to learn to negotiate stairs. Other decisions are judgment calls. All are the product of the interplay between parent and child. Pressing for greater autonomy and freedom, children require their parents to calibrate each request against their knowledge of the individual child, their values, and their own readiness to let go. For all families, this ongoing deliberation is both taxing and challenging. For families with a disabled child, the process is complicated by several factors.

First, the "blueprint" of normative development that gives parents a reference point to other children may not apply to a disabled child. Parents of disabled children report that the diagnosis took away their expectation of "normal" development, leaving them without guidelines and with reduced confidence, at least for a time, in their parenting. No doubt, the heavy dose of professional expertise that most families with a disabled child receive also erodes parental confidence.

Second, parents of disabled children are more likely to become stalled in a pattern of overprotection toward their children. A difficult birth, medical conditions that increase the severity of any illness or injury, or unfortunate negative reactions from family or friends prime parents to guard their child closely. In addition, parents with a disabled child may themselves be more protected from routine feedback about their parenting from their social network.

Third, as noted earlier, the press for change in parental behavior and family rules generally comes from the developing child. Children with disabilities often press for such change with less fervor, particularly those whose interactions with peers have been restricted. Peers often provide children with the support and the models that they need to alter family rules and obtain new, appropriate privileges.

When this delicate balance of parenting goes awry, the family therapist must evaluate the input of both the parents and the children in determining where to intervene. In many families, a disabled child's immature behavior or reticent stance can be challenged: "What! You still let your mother pick out your clothes? I guess you need her to keep you young." Other children learn the skills

needed to negotiate with their families through coaching, both in enactments around concrete issues with their families and in individual role playing with the therapist. By challenging disabled children to exhibit more mature behavior or teaching them new skills, the therapist empowers them to change the family pattern.

In order to work effectively through the child in altering the parent-child relationship, the focus must remain very concrete, and the child must be motivated to remain engaged long enough for the interaction pattern to change. Therefore, when coaching a reticent child to challenge parental limits, the therapist must select a specific issue in which the child is interested.

The family of a very quiet and compliant child with learning disabilities and recurrent somatic complaints was organized protectively around him. His mother always walked with him to the bus stop, kept track of his belongings, and assisted him onto the bus. After several unsuccessful probes by the therapist, the boy showed an interest in boarding the school bus alone. Altering this small piece of the mother-child interaction was the first step in shifting their relationship toward a developmentally more appropriate pattern.

Sometimes, young children can be motivated to change by the tactic of betting.

A bright, visually handicapped 6-year-old had developed a severe problem of dawdling in the morning. The parents were very aggravated, but consistently succumbed to her helpless pleas and gave her much more assistance with self-care tasks than she needed in order to get her to school on time. The therapist first expressed doubt that she really could do such tasks as comb her hair, put on her socks, and wash her face; the therapist then insisted that she demonstrate each skill, which she did with growing glee as she proved the therapist wrong. This demonstration allowed the therapist to evaluate the child's actual skill level and to assess her parents' tolerance of her pace and methods. Although the child did most tasks reasonably well, the therapist remained pessimistic. The therapist and the child then arranged a formal bet, focusing on a specific time for the child to be ready for school, and they agreed that she would call the next day to let the therapist know who had won. No rewards or punishers were used except the therapist's continued pessimism and chagrin at her success. The bet was reiterated for 2 or 3 weeks until the problem was forgotten. The intervention redirected the child's struggle away from the parents and toward the therapist, capitalizing on her competitive spirit.

Working through a child to produce change in a family's interactions is a good tactic if the therapist is comfortable with children, knowledgeable about developmental tasks, and willing to be playful. Moreover, it is a gentle way to effect change in a family. When parents are sensitive to professional opinion about their parenting, maximizing the child's energy for change minimizes the parents' resistance.

The Petersons were referred for therapy by the director of the preschool that their 5-year-old daughter attended. Melissa, who had been born prematurely, had a seizure disorder, attentional deficits, and speech and language problems. She had severe problems separating from her parents and was having tantrums at school. There were many indications of an enmeshed family structure. Her father, who took her to school, was cueing and reinforcing considerable dependent behavior in the morning. His office was across the street from the school, and he and Melissa typically arrived early to eat breakfast at his firm's cafeteria. Then he would *carry* Melissa across the street to school. Because of his own history, which included a number of losses and "cut-offs," he was particularly attached to Melissa and anxious about leaving her each morning.

Although the teachers had changed their response to Melissa's behavior at school, it was necessary to change the father-child interaction before school in order to set a different tone for the school day. Rather than address the father's behavior to break the sequence, the therapist chose an intervention that challenged Melissa to more age-appropriate behavior. Expressing dismay that her father was "jaywalking" when he carried Melissa across the street, the therapist asked her to "teach" her father how to cross with the traffic light. She and the therapist rehearsed what she would need to do to help her father "learn" to cross the street more safely. Absorbed in the task, both Melissa and her father viewed their leave-taking differently.

Because their confidence in their parenting may be shaken by the diagnosis of disability, parents may need assistance not only with their disabled child, but also with their nondisabled children. Occasionally, the therapist must support parents in dealing with issues that they have handled competently in the past.

A couple that had successfully raised one child to adulthood sought therapy because they believed that their 14-year-old, normally developing child was "out of control," manipulative, and unwilling to put forth her best efforts at school. The girl had been well adjusted both at home and at school until she reached adolescence. The couple's third child had Down's syndrome, and they were quite anxious about this child. The identified patient was simply testing her parents' limits (not uncommon in adolescence), and the parents were responding inconsistently. The task of the therapist was to draw analogies between the symptomatic child and her older sister, thus confirming the parents' competence to deal with familiar patterns of behavior.

MULTIPLE SERVICE SYSTEMS AND HELPING PROFESSIONALS

Children with disabilities and their families are typically involved with a variety of different service systems and professionals. A child with a disability may have several medical doctors, work with special education teachers, and receive services from a speech, physical, or occupational therapist, as well as a psychologist. To ignore the child's involvement with this network of other professionals is unwise.

The extent of the family's involvement with other service systems may correlate with the family's availability and commitment to family therapy. Many families with a disabled child balance an incredible array of appointments, and therapy must be immediately helpful to be perceived as worth the time commitment. The perspective of these other professionals on the problem should be investigated, as it may reveal useful frames and tactics. For example, occupational therapists can recommend several modifications of a child's clothing to facilitate self-dressing, which fits nicely with the therapy goal of increasing the child's autonomy. When the child becomes more independent in self-care tasks, the parents may be better able to see a readiness for independence in other areas. In investigating other professionals' viewpoints, the therapist must remember that triangles involving family members and other helping professionals are not uncommon (Carl & Jurkovic, 1983; Foster, 1984).

Therapists should consider using a number of settings as contexts for treatment (Berger & Jurkovic, 1984) and should become familiar with the language and methods of other professions in order to achieve family therapy goals. Adopting this perspective broadens the therapist's profile as a change agent considerably, but requires abandoning the assumption that the consulting room is the locus for change. For example, the classic family structure with an enmeshed mother-child pair and a disengaged father is a pattern often perpetuated by professionals working exclusively with mothers and children (Foster & Berger, 1979). An alternative or adjunct to traditional family therapy is for the family therapist to work through the network of involved helping professionals. For a family working with a physical therapist, for example, tasks to include the father in the physical therapy program may be given. Many allied health professionals are receptive to such suggestions, and therapists who have adopted this approach have learned much about other professions that has been useful in their own work with families with disabled children. This model may be particularly valuable for clinicians who work in multidisciplinary settings, such as clinics or hospitals, but it is also appropriate for therapists in independent practice who are willing to do the groundwork with the other professionals (see Foster & Berger, 1979; Foster, Berger, & McLean, 1981). This way of thinking and working holds promise as a preventive measure as well.

From the child's perspective, involvement with a network of professionals may be either negative or positive. Some children, usually older ones, resent these nonvoluntary therapy routines and appointments, and they resist carrying out prescribed programs. When compliance is a problem, the issue of autonomy may underlie it. The child may be acquiring appropriate autonomy in other areas (e.g., homework, clothes, chores), but the treatment of the disability may still be negotiated between parents and professionals. Although many professionals are superb at including the child in treatment planning, not all recognize a child's readiness to be included. Parental overprotection may also cloud the process. The family therapist can reframe the resistance as an awkward signal of the child's desire for more choices and can work directly with the adults to alter the treatment approach. For example, preadolescents enjoy being offered choices about appointment times or therapy regimes. These children can be challenged to find out about their disability and their treatment plan, as well as to stand up and be heard when they feel that the adults are excluding them from the decision-making process.

One 11-year-old with spina bifida disliked his urologist and resisted most medical appointments. After being coached by the therapist, he asked the physician some questions while his parents were out of the room. The physician responded seriously to the boy's inquiries, and the experience gave the boy a sense of greater involvement in his treatment. The boy confided later that he "still didn't like him," but he felt better about going to the clinic.

For some disabled children, particularly those excluded from many peer activities, the professional network is an important source of social contact and self-esteem. Relationships with helping professionals, like peer relationships, can help the child bridge the gap between family and the larger world. Unlike peer relationships, however, they are not between equals, and they are often nonvoluntary. Furthermore, patterns of adultification or infantilization are occasionally perpetuated in professional-child relationships, and the child often has problems relating to peers. While an obvious tactic is to increase the child's opportunities for contact with peers, it may also be helpful to block the child's inappropriate interactions with professionals.

A 10-year-old girl with brain damage as a result of encephalitis was bossy and prissy with her peers. Her reading and verbal skills were well above average, but her math and spatial skills were very weak. Her parents reinforced her verbal prowess, set few limits, and generally expressed amazement that she was doing so well. Although the child desperately wanted friends, she turned them away by her behavior. She was very close to her occupational therapist, whom she saw weekly. Like her parents, this therapist reinforced the child's adultified, verbal style. Concurrent with the family therapy (in which the pace of change was very slow), the family therapist worked with the occupational therapist to block adultified behavior in the girl; essentially, this involved disrupting the "peer" relationship made possible by the girl's verbal competence and reinstating a hierarchy between them. While this was but one part of a therapy directed toward establishing the girl in peer relationships, it was critical—given the family's reluctance to treat her differently.

Family therapists working with young disabled children may need to function in roles other than that of therapist in order to help families find their way through the maze of different service systems. At times, the therapist must function as a case manager, helping the parents acquire needed services or setting priorities for treatment goals. Familiarity with the child's educational, medical, and therapeutic needs; knowledge of available community services; and the ability to communicate effectively with the other professionals involved is critical if the family therapist is to assume this role. Furthermore, as the person with the broadest perspective on the system, the family therapist is best able to guide a family in reconciling disparate opinions and determining treatment priorities that take into account the needs of the whole family. Assisting a family in balancing such issues is often an important therapeutic goal.

Occasionally, therapists must become child or family advocates, taking a stand with a family against a service system, another professional, or a social policy. This is similar to an unbalancing move in therapy, in which the therapist sides with one person or subsystem against another.

In one family with a learning-disabled child, school system personnel were subtly pressuring the parents to agree to a particular special education placement. The test data were outdated and equivocal. The parents were unaware of their legal rights and due process under Pub. L. 94-142 regarding special education placement. The therapist took a strong position against the school system's recommendation and supported the parents in demanding a new assessment and another conference to determine placement.

By taking such an advocacy role the therapist can place a family in an adversarial position in relation to another service system. When the family must continue to work with this service system after the difference is settled, the therapist should help the family members work through their feelings about the dispute and achieve a cooperative working relationship once more. The key to this process is the therapist's willingness to resume a position of relative neutrality vis-à-vis the family and other systems.

CONCLUSION

For too long in the field of family therapy, the baby has been thrown out with the bath water of individual child treatment. Understanding the child's perspective and working directly with the individual child within a family or community context is consistent with a systems way of thinking and working, however. Moreover, for families with disabled children, it seems particularly crucial that therapists show themselves to be competent and comfortable in working with the children. Therapy is a reflection of our culture and its values and attitudes, and the therapist who chooses to work with disabled children only through the parents, however successfully, must question whether such a practice derives from a therapeutic model or from cultural conditioning to avoid the disabled.

REFERENCES

Berger, M., & Jurkovic, G.J. (Eds.). (1984). *Practicing family therapy in diverse settings*. San Francisco: Jossey Bass.

Carl, D., & Jurkovic, G.J. (1983). Agency triangles: Problems in agency-family relationships. *Family Process, 22,* 441–452.

Foster, M.A. (1984). Schools. In M. Berger & G.J. Jurkovic (Eds.), *Practicing family therapy in diverse settings* (pp. 110-141). San Francisco: Jossey Bass.

Foster, M., & Berger, M. (1979). Structural family therapy: Applications in programs for preschool handicapped children. *Journal of the Early Childhood, 1,* 52–58.

Foster, M.A., & Berger, M. (1985). Research with families with handicapped children: A multilevel systemic perspective. In L. L'Abate (Ed.), *Handbook of family psychology and family therapy* Vol. 1. Homewood, IL: Dorsey Press.

Foster, M.A., Berger, M., & McLean, J. (1981). Rethinking a good idea: A reassessment of parent involvement. *Topics in Early Childhood Special Education, 1,* 55–65.

Gardner, R.A. (1971). *Therapeutic communication with children: The mutual storytelling technique*. New York: Jason Aronson.

8

Treating Young Children from Seriously Dysfunctional Family Systems

William R. Seelig, MSW, LCSW
Clinical Director
Eastfield Children's Center
Campbell, California

THE EASTFIELD CHILDREN'S Center is a private, nonprofit mental health center that is committed to the treatment of seriously disturbed children and adolescents within the context of their family, community, and cultural systems. Most of the children referred to the center's intensive services have multiple problems. Some have serious learning handicaps or developmental difficulties. Many have experienced neglect and physical or sexual abuse. They often find it difficult to make attachments and have defensive behavioral repertoires that promote distance, maintain conflictual dependencies, and/or serve the needs of their family systems. Most associate school with failure, and a number have a history of unsuccessful prior placements.

The families of these children usually have multiple problems as well. Some exhibit intergenerational patterns of chaos or enmeshment. Others are fragmented, disengaged, or isolated. Many of these families are not meeting their members' basic needs for nurturance, safety, or stimulation. Others meet these needs only on occasion or with highly neurotic or psychotic behavioral patterning.

CHILDREN AND FAMILIES IN EVOLUTION

The systems thinking and the related clinical model used at the Eastfield Children's Center have been evolving over the past 7 years. It has been drawn from the work of the author and the experience of the staff and from the efforts of others in child and family mental health (Bowen, 1978; Carter & McGoldrick, 1980; Haley, 1980; Hoffman, 1980;

Minuchin & Fishman, 1981; Terkelson, 1980).

Change: Transformation vs. Symptomatic Patterning

The family's structure and organization set the context within which the child and the related subsystem develop. It provides a climate of expectations, challenges, and supports in relation to developmental needs. As the child or the related subsystem eventually masters new tasks and begins adapting to the next developmental phase, the family structure changes.

Any family system initially will try to adapt to changes with its usual responses; when this fails, the family develops ad hoc measures to cope. When neither of these approaches leads to successful adaptation, the family becomes increasingly irritable and, eventually, goes into a state of confusion or crisis. Healthy families have enough tenacity to provide basic safety and stimulation, as well as sufficient internal resources to provide nurturance, during this period of trial, error, and instability. Somewhere in the midst of this process, the family makes a major shift or "leap," to a new level of integration. The family makes a basic structural shift, the child moves developmentally, and the family system "transforms." This step in the family's evolutionary process is successful. In these family systems, the structure meets needs, bringing increased flexibility, more options, and an expanded world view. The child and related subsystem are increasingly confident and enjoy a solid sense of self and a sense of belonging.

Families troubled by past injunctions or overwhelmed by current problems or

crises frequently do not complete this developmental cycle. In some, the child is given and/or senses the troubled pulse of the system and responds in a symptomatic, attention-diverting manner. In other cases, the family supports the child into the beginning of a developmental "transformation," but becomes anxious and discounts the whole event, leaving the child intensely disorganized and symptomatic. This systemic process also redirects the family's energies and calms the broader system. Many of these families remain stalled, and the symptomatic child has ever-increasing difficulties. In these dysfunctional families, the structure fails to meet childhood needs, rigidity is increased, and there is a pervasive sense of "stuckness." Their world view and options contract or remain unchanged. The child misses or only partially accomplishes critical early milestones, developing symptoms in lieu of basic skills and increased competence. The child may feel either rejected or engulfed and is left with a poor sense of self.

Challenging Families to Evolve

When young children are referred for treatment of a condition labeled as a severe emotional and/or behavioral disturbance, it can be assumed that both child and family have failed to transform developmentally. Failure in the early stages brings both a systemic "stuckness" and an individual vulnerability and defensiveness that is often difficult to treat. Bonding and attachment problems are particularly complex, as are psychogenic complications. The parent(s) may have been labeled psychotic, borderline psychotic, addicted, or seriously depressed. The lack of family resources often mandates some form of placement for both safety and continuing intervention. The therapist has the task of joining with both the child and the family in the least restrictive, but workable, therapeutic format to challenge them toward positive transformation. The goal is the maximization of individual and family system resources and competencies toward a more functional, developmental evolution.

THERAPEUTIC SYSTEMS FOR WORKING WITH SERIOUSLY DYSFUNCTIONAL FAMILIES

While the basic goal is to keep young children within their own nuclear or extended family system, many children need therapeutic placement. At Eastfield Children's Center, family-oriented residential treatment and school-based day treatment systems have been established for use in these situations. Whatever the placement, much attention is given to family values and belief systems at the center. There is a deep belief in the ability of families to draw on their "own" resources to parent their children or to make intelligent, caring decisions about substitute parenting environments. Because of a firm belief that parents and, in turn, children, can change, we expect our staff to go to great lengths to challenge each toward increased competence.

Therapeutic Teams: Complex, Healthy Systems

Working with young children who have multiple difficulties and their troubled parents is a many faceted task. At the center, therefore, we use therapeutic teams in both the residential and day treatment programs. Both programs are operated in small-group formats under the clinical/administrative direction of a unit supervisor. A child psychiatrist is available for systemic and child-focused consultation on a weekly basis. Other clinical and educational resources are available when needed. Each unit supervisor is responsible for the development and maintenance of the health of each therapeutic team. These teams are expected to actively engage and challenge both child and family with the goal of individual and systems change. The creation of warm, nurturing environments with high standards and expectations for persistent personal and group growth is critical. Much effort goes into the maintenance of a flexible but clear team structure and an open, dynamic process between team members. This affords a rich array of competencies and the interpersonal strength to recognize, withstand and move beyond the tremendous inductive pulls of the children and families served in each setting.

Residential Treatment

Cottage teams of therapists run a 24-hour therapeutic milieu designed to provide quality care and to move children who need residential treatment toward healthier, less conflictual interpersonal relationships with peers and adults. Teaching basic life and play skills, remediating in deficit areas, and expanding potentials are important in this process. Daily coordination with the school and weekly consultation with the families are included. The on-grounds school is staffed by special education professionals who provide both group and individualized educational programming. This includes a great deal of remedial work for learning disabilities or major educational deficits. Whenever possible, children are home each weekend. Each child's key milieu therapist participates in family treatment and coordinates the visiting process. Both school and milieu environments are designed to prepare children for "community" life.

The social workers at the center are responsible for engaging all parents in family treatment. They try to use the child's residential placement as an opportunity for parental empowerment, parental involvement as peers in the milieu and special education process, family restructuring and change, and parental reunification or, when necessary, parent-facilitated placement in an alternate family setting. They frequently use other therapeutic formats as well (e.g., child, marital, multigenerational and multiple family therapy). Outreach is aggressive.

Day Treatment

School-based teams of therapists run daylong activity/therapy programs in close conjunction with special education classes. These programs are integrated into elementary and junior high schools and are more normalized than are the residential programs. They are open throughout the year, including school vacations and holidays. Their intensity is similar to that of the residential programs, and they include a similar array of interventions. Activity therapy in relation to each child's functioning in the classroom, on the playground, and in family settings is stressed. Opportunities for mainstreaming are maximized. There

is daily communication with parents. Social workers within the program are responsible for family therapy and parental involvement; their basic goals are similar to those of their colleagues in the residential programs.

Linkages with Larger Systems

The development of effective working linkages with larger systems is the key to success or failure with these children and their families. The power of a placing agency, the court, the police, or child protective services can often be used to build intensity with families that are stalled in abusive, neglecting, or avoidant patterns. The unpredictability and the escalation of the behavior of both children and parents at times forces the use of acute hospital or subacute residential programs for basic safety and protection. Furthermore, enlisting the ongoing support of the agencies that provide the actual payment for care requires us to support them in return. They are also stressed, and they need respect, understanding, and room to fulfill their unique responsibilities. Given this approach, most will join with therapeutic centers in developing complementary plans for intervention.

CASE EXAMPLE: ATTEMPTED SUICIDE IN A VOLATILE FAMILY SYSTEM*

Henry was 7 years old when referred to the Eastfield Children's Center by an inpatient unit in another city. He

Note: The following cases were treated in our center over the past two years. I served as a family consultant on the first. Mark Mendelow, LCSW, was the primary therapist with this family. I served as a consultant and clinical supervisor on the second. Melanie Pla-Richard, LCSW, was the unit supervisor and primary therapist with this family. The staffs on the respective teams and the family members deserve primary credit.

had attempted to hang himself 4 months earlier and had been cyanotic when his sister discovered him. He was described as deeply depressed with little self-esteem. When not stressed, he could be cheerful; when frustrated, he could quickly explode into a rage, screaming, hitting walls, and saying that everyone was against him. This rage would progress to broader themes of worthlessness ("I'm a piece of shit"), and he would wish that he were dead and could kill himself. Henry's mother, Bette, had a complex history and labeled herself manic-depressive. His natural father was categorized as psychotic, and his stepfather, Andy, was purported to have a cocaine problem. The court had taken custody of Henry for treatment purposes, and the family was referred to the center's residential program for child and family treatment.

The family arrived en masse, an hour late for their first appointment. Andy, aged 36; Bette, aged 34; Sam, aged 12; Henry, aged 7; Judy, aged 4; and Jane, aged 2, attended.

Bette began, reluctantly, saying that she could not handle Henry's problem all by herself. Andy was away most of the time. She felt that there were deep psychological problems in the family and that these problems had hurt Henry and could hurt others. Andy felt that Henry was just sensitive and insecure. Henry said that a "bad spirit" inside him caused him to act the way he did.

Both spouses had prior marriages that they described as unsuccessful. There was little contact in this regard, even in relation to the children. A brief diagram of the Smith family follows (see Figure 1).

At the time of therapy, Bette was estranged from her family of origin. She described herself as the "family failure," having had numerous emotional problems throughout her life. Because she had made her first suicide attempt when she was Henry's age, she identified with his anger and depression. She appeared to cling to her manic-depressive label and lithium/anti-depressant therapy for protection and distance. Bette seemed overreactive to Henry and

Figure 1 The Smith Family Diagram

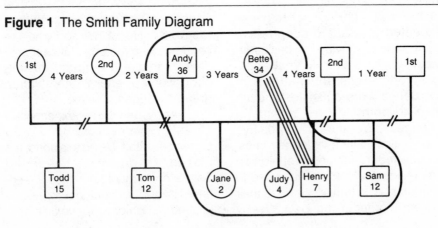

underreactive to the other three children. Although struggling as a parent, she worked from her home and basically supported the family. Andy was struggling with his family business and found little time for the family. He evidently avoided family problems through drugs and sporadic affairs. The couple described their marriage as conflicted, with frequent separations. The younger children had a needy, chaotic quality. Sam was parental in this regard, although he was also depressed.

This family had serious individual and hierarchical problems. The adults were chronically cut off from their extended families and from each other. Henry appeared to be enmeshed with his mother and triangled into the marital discord. His struggle seemed to be both internal and systemically protective in nature. Family structure and nurturance seemed inconsistent, with periods of rage or intense emotionality common.

The goals for therapy were numerous. Henry's placement was used to nurture him, support him, and eventually to challenge his negative view of himself. The parents were expected to assume cooperative control and to provide the basic nurturance within the family. Their negative world views and patterns of avoidance were consistently challenged, both directly and metaphorically, by means of positive expectations, empowering reframes, and boundary-making techniques. The residential context was used to support and, in turn, destabilize their system in order to change it. Weekly

family therapy sessions and weekends at home maintained active family involvement in Henry's treatment and allowed for practice and eventual transformation.

During the first 6 months, parenting and marital issues had priority. Henry continued to vacillate between excellent behavior and unpredictable outbursts in school, in the milieu, and at home. He was somewhat responsive to paradoxical interventions, but even these were only partially successful. He still needed to keep people on edge and distant. Andy once again began staying away during the week, leaving Bette with the bulk of the parenting. In addition, Sam began to misbehave at school during this period.

The therapeutic team insisted that both parents could and should take control. As the team pushed them, their underlying marital problems surfaced and contaminated their parenting work. The therapists were prematurely inducted into a trial of direct marital therapy, which only exacerbated the marital conflict. When this failed, the therapists challenged the couple to put the marital issues aside in order to work together to save the "life" of their son, who had once again made suicidal gestures. This intensive, boundary-making effort worked, and all the children gradually began to relax.

As Andy and Bette experienced parenting successes, Bette grew close to the staff. Using this bond, the therapists directly challenged Bette's concept of herself as a mentally ill, incompetent person. They labeled her emotionally volatile periods and her depressed periods as "choices she had made" in response to difficult situations rather than "internal givens." Although upset with the therapists, she eventually made sound decisions and developed a plan to avoid self-injury during her periods of depression. Fortunately, she loathed the police and inpatient unit, which was the last resort if she continued in a self-injurious mode. Bette subsequently took control of these situations and independently stopped taking her medications without negative result. Because she was no longer paralyzed by her own fears, Bette was able to challenge Henry in a much more direct, differentiated fashion to control himself. Bette's confident, eye-to-eye confrontation of Henry triggered a major transformation in their relationship. Henry had been given a congruent message to believe in himself; therefore, he could surrender much of his unpredictability and move closer to adults and peers.

The distance between Bette and Andy increased, and they separated again. The therapists' suspicions about his drug involvement grew. As Bette struggled with this problem, the therapists urged her to invite her estranged parents as consultants to the therapeutic process. She did, and they were quite helpful. When asked for their ideas on how Bette might more successfully approach Andy, or men in general, Bette's parents shared an array of very personal experiences from their own marriage. These practical, homespun approaches were touching to all

involved. After Bette agreed that she would not shut them out in anger, they shared their observations on what both she and Andy might do to improve their relationship. Bette and her mother agreed to talk more often, and they have done so. Shortly after this, Bette began attending Al-Anon meetings regularly. She was still unsure about her relationship with Andy, preferring to proceed slowly before making decisions.

Henry was in the center's residential program for 16 months. With the help of family and staff, he became more open to genuine involvements. He carried himself like a miniature John Wayne, challenging authority and peers, and simultaneously discussing his feelings and fears. He began to feel good about himself, to take risks, and to assume responsibilities. He was well-liked both by staff and by other children. There was, however, still much work for Henry and his family to do. All agreed that a transitional stay in day treatment would be the best route home. The family is continuing to work in this setting.

CASE EXAMPLE: FIRESETTING IN A MULTIGENERATIONAL CONTEXT

Steve was 7 years old at the time of his referral by a local school district. His teachers described him as a hyperactive boy whose extremely antisocial behavior included lying, verbal attacks, and physical abuse of other children. He had set two serious fires, the first of which had burned his paternal grandmother's house to the ground. His grandmother, Glenda, had taken him for a brief period of therapy, which resulted in a trial of methylphenidate hydrochloride (Ritalin). She terminated this effort, however, and had recently refused a referral for residential treatment. A second fire, together with escalating school problems and behavior problems at home, provided the impetus for Steve's referral to the day treatment program at Eastfield Children's Center.

Glenda, Steve, and George, Steve's father, appeared for the initial session. Glenda was a matronly woman in her early 50s who took charge of the session by prompting and directing both her son and her grandson. A rugged cowboy type, George was both rebellious and deferential to his mother. At one point, he said, "You can't argue with Mom. She's like a drill sergeant." Steve was a well-dressed, good-looking child who was closely aligned with his grandmother, but distant from his father. Describing Steve as bossy, argumentative, and defiant, Glenda wanted him to change. George agreed, but seemed less willing to take action. Steve blocked his ears and in a manipulative fashion said, "Grandma doesn't like me." She, of course, reacted. Both Glenda and George seemed inappropriately casual about the serious fires that Steve had set.

In exploring the broader family system, the therapeutic team found a series of conflicted, alcohol-related marriages and major separation problems in George's generation (see Figure 2, the Jones Family diagram). Glenda was talking about a divorce from her current husband. George was having work and marital difficulties. His siblings had varying problems and were in and out of the home, as were numerous boarders. Steve seemed to be receiving inconsistent parenting and was probably experiencing rejection and neglect.

This three-generation family appeared to be seriously enmeshed and unable to develop more differentiated marital or parenting relationships. Glenda clung to her role as care-giver with spouses, children, and grandchildren. Others in the family avoided individuation by maintaining a helpless dependency or by exhibiting behavior problems. Steve's behavior problems not only brought adult attention and concern, but also provided a continued focus for the larger system. Steve's fire-setting was symbolic in this regard. He set the house ablaze when his uncle was being taken from the home to be incarcerated for seriously injuring someone in a fight.

The therapeutic goal was to challenge the family to maintain its focus on Steve, to provide the consistent nurturance and guidance that he desperately needed, and simultaneously to use these processes to restructure and transform the larger family system. Throughout treatment, the therapists expected and demanded that the family assist the day treatment staff in their work with Steve. The maintenance of a warm, caring, goal-oriented milieu/educational program in which competence was expected to increase was both

Figure 2 The Jones Family Diagram

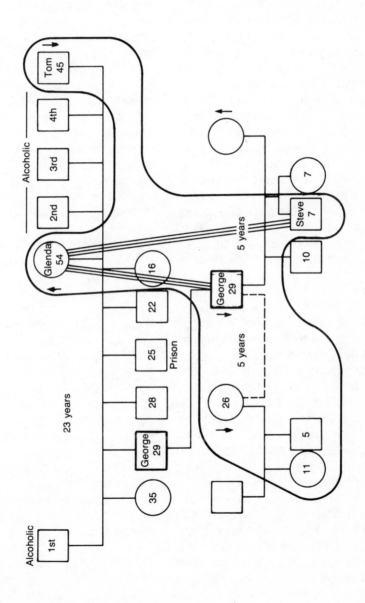

enticing and unsettling to the family. It allowed the therapists constant access to the broader family and the related family issues that maintained their intergenerational dysfunction.

In the early months of treatment, the therapists focused on joining with Glenda to support her adult son, George, in the resumption of more responsibilities in parenting Steve. Although there was some progress in this regard, George's dependency on Glenda soon surfaced as a major issue. The initial success and positive potentials were then used as a context within which to approach this larger problem. With support, positive reframes, and increased intensity, Glenda and her husband, Ted, were able to establish a schedule for George's move from their home. They shared similar experiences in their lives with him and offered to assist him. Although angered and belligerent because he was being told to move, George did, in fact, move out with his mate and her two children within 2 months. They did not sever connections with Glenda, but for the first time, they did not rely on her for economic assistance. Steve stayed with Glenda.

In the following months, Steve made consistent progress in the program; however, he remained reactive to continuing incidents in the family. George participated in some planned events with his son, but seemed less available and more involved in economic and spousal concerns. In a nonrejecting manner, he began to question the feasibility of his plan to assume the major responsibility for Steve's care. With George

functioning on his own and Steve improving within the program, Glenda's marital problems came to the fore. Ted's drinking continued, and the time that he spent away from home increased. Embarrassed and upset, Glenda began avoiding therapy. With persistent support outreach and sessions in her home, Glenda was reinvolved in treatment. She eventually persuaded Ted to attend a brief series of sessions to assess the future of their marriage, although he was fairly resistant to involvement. His drinking continued, as did his extramarital liaisons. Glenda obtained an amicable divorce and allowed Ted some continuing grandfathering contacts with Steve.

Glenda entered a 6-month phase of therapy in which she began seriously to examine her overfunctioning, care-giving role in life. From 9 years of age to her 16th birthday, Glenda had cared for her invalid mother. Then she had begun a family as a teen-aged mother. With constant support and cajoling, Glenda finally began to focus on her personal needs and on the development of a female support system. Eventually, she took her first personal vacation in many years. Glenda's relationships with men shifted. She purchased a service station, established a no drinking rule, and hired men who were more independently responsible.

Glenda's relationship with her son, George, and his mate also improved. They began to work together in matters that involved Steve and even joined forces in a ceremony to discard Steve's "School Is the Pits" T-shirt to demonstrate their support for the program and their joint expectations for Steve. They also arranged a highly successful summer visit with Steve for his natural mother, his twin sister, and his older brother. The family's visit to the program on Steve's return, with Steve as tour guide, was the highlight of that summer's experience.

Steve was now almost 9 and had not "played" with matches in more than a year. His relations with adults were excellent. He sought praise and recognition, even though he still found it difficult to handle them. Although he was occasionally manipulative and told a few white lies, he was liked by his peers. Steve "knew" he could do his schoolwork and was proud of it. He was less reactive to external stressors and had become a more differentiated child who was identifying with and internalizing the values and goals of the family and staff. After 18 months in day treatment, Steve returned to his community school with the support of his grandmother and extended family. There were some incidents, but more successes. The following summer, Glenda, George, and Steve's natural mother jointly decided to grant Steve's wish to live with his mother. He visits his grandmother and his father, and he appears to be doing as well as any 9-year-old.

CONCLUSION

Treating small children with serious problems is a difficult and time-consuming task. Treating their seriously dysfunctional families greatly complicates the undertaking. Many therapists in the business of helping children are convinced that it is not prudent to do one without the other, however. The advent of systemic thinking in mental health, the growth and integration of family and child treatment models, and the ever-expanding potpourri of related techniques makes it possible to organize a complex array of data into working hypotheses, relate these to core structures or processes for change, and proceed. We can't, however, make life simpler or determine when or how these complex families will transform or in which direction they might go in the weeks or months ahead. All we can do is develop our best hypotheses, define core goals for system change and be prepared to creatively join with and challenge these families from multiple perspectives. It is frequently a long journey for staff and for those they serve. With the right beliefs, expectations, and supports, it can be a successful and transforming experience for both.

REFERENCES

Bowen, M. (1978). *Family therapy in clinical practice*. New York: Jason Aronson.

Carter, E., & McGoldrick, M. (Eds.). (1980). *The family life cycle: A framework for family therapy*. New York: Gardner Press.

Haley, J. (1980). *Leaving home: The therapy of disturbed young people*. New York: McGraw-Hill.

Hoffman, L. (1980). The family life cycle and discontinuous change. In E. Carter & M. McGoldrick (Eds.), *The family life cycle: A framework for family therapy* (pp. 53–68). New York: Gardner Press.

Minuchin, S., & Fishman, C. (1981). *Family therapy techniques*. Cambridge, MA: Harvard University Press.

Terkelson, K. (1980). Toward a theory of the family life cycle. In E. Carter & M. McGoldrick (Eds.), *The family life cycle: A framework for family therapy* (pp. 21–52). New York: Gardner Press.

9

The Treatment of Hospitalized Families of Young Children

John Brendler, ACSW
Associate Clinical Director
Child and Family Inpatient Service
Philadelphia Child Guidance Clinic
Philadelphia, Pennsylvania

Lee Combrinck-Graham, MD
Director, Master of Family Therapy
  Program
Mental Health Sciences
Hahnemann University
Philadelphia, Pennsylvania

F AMILIES WITH CHILDREN who exhibit serious, chronic behavior problems that have not responded to therapy in conventional outpatient and inpatient settings may be candidates for hospitalization as a family. The apartment program of the Philadelphia Child Guidance Clinic, for example, is designed to provide intensive treatment to whole families to help them deal with the most difficult of their children's problems. Such problems include child abuse and neglect, school avoidance, truancy, running away, firesetting, suicide attempts, psychosis, and psychosomatic disorders (e.g., intractable asthma and diabetes with recurring ketoacidosis).

These families have frequently been labeled unworkable or resistant to therapy. They generally feel overwhelmed and depleted. Everyone involved with them feels stuck. At the time of referral, many of the children are facing placement in long-term care institutions. Often, their parents have been perceived as incompetent and destructive, and the symptomatic children have been designated as emotionally ill. Because these families are desperate for relief, they may be willing to abandon their usual ways of living and attempt extraordinary modifications in their ways of being together. Such families often view hospitalization as a last resort. Family members enter the hospital prepared to work intensively in a last-ditch effort to reorganize their lives to save their children and their families (Brendler, 1983).

At the outset, it is essential to activate the families' appreciation of themselves as resources. The hospital treatment can be used to create contexts that promote parental competence, clear and permeable personal and generational boundaries, mechanisms for conflict resolution, cooperation between family members, and individual competence. Four central themes shape treatment in the apartment program: (1) constructing a context for functional change, (2) making symptoms work for the family, (3) focusing on parents as parents, and (4) enhancing playfulness.

Over the past 6 years, approximately 200 families have been treated in the apartments at the Philadelphia Child Guidance Clinic, each family staying in an apartment for an average of 20 days. A special interdisciplinary team works with the apartment families.

CONSTRUCTING A THERAPEUTIC CONTEXT

No matter what the model is, creating a context in which the patients (in this case, the family) can explore different ways of viewing their worlds and of solving problems is fundamental to the process of therapy.

A state of crisis is often an important condition for change (Langsley & Kaplan, 1968). Although having severely symptomatic children may seem to constitute a crisis sufficient to motivate most families to change, many of these families are so chronically stressed and so accustomed to living with symptoms that they do not perceive the symptomatic behaviors as indications of a crisis. For many, the hospitalization itself is a crisis (Combrinck-Graham, 1985). In moving from home to hospital, the family moves to a new culture, temporarily abandoning its usual routines to enter a world of new faces, new surroundings, new rules, and even new language. The family members are not familiar with the program, so they must ask about everything.

In this state of disequilibrium, suspended between the old and familiar and the new and strange, the family appears to be most receptive to new ideas and ready to experiment with new behaviors. At this point, the staff tries to initiate the family's reorganization. Because the staff attempts to join the family in a way that highlights family strengths, the family usually connects quickly to what must seem to be the only stable offering in an otherwise bewildering situation (Anderson, 1977; Brendler, 1983).

The M. family consists of two parents and 10-year-old Billy. Mr. M. is blind, deaf, and mute; Mrs. M. is deaf and mute. Billy hears, speaks, and knows how to sign. At home, Billy had temper tantrums and was physically violent toward both his parents when he did not get his way.

Mr. and Mrs. M. could not manage Billy. He capitalized on their physical handicaps and terrorized them at will. The family seemed to need a drastically different experience in order to learn to provide more direction and support for their child.

Many of these families have been very dependent on societal institutions, and the hospitalization could accentuate their dependency (Bowen, 1966; Grunebaum & Weiss, 1963; Nakhla, Folkart, & Webster, 1969). The staff counters this by expecting families to manage their children more effectively right from the start. Because the children, too, are bewildered by this change in family life, they are likely to respond to different handling by their parents. Thus, new possibilities emerge from the confusion as the family is placed in charge and learns to use its own resources and those of its surrounding community more competently. (At first, of course, the hospital staff is the surrounding community) (Combrinck-Graham, Gursky & Brendler, 1982).

As soon as the M. family was admitted to the apartment, a staff person joined the family for the express purpose of protecting the parents from Billy. It was not long before the parents' best friends, also deaf, were invited to join a family therapy session. The friends announced their willingness to help the M. family and berated Billy for his outrageous behavior. As the third step in enlarging the family's experience of community resources, a policeman from the district in which the family lived was invited to a session. The policeman read the riot act to Billy and notified him of the legal consequences of any further assaults on his parents. Following this, the family and the therapeutic team went to the police station where Billy, alone, was taken on a tour to familiarize him with the surroundings to which he would be confined if he continued to beat or threaten his parents (Castaneda, 1972). Billy quickly responded by stopping the tantrums and violent behavior.

The therapists made no effort to control Billy or to teach him how to behave. Instead, they encouraged him in his efforts to relate to his parents. Once he had more control of his behavior, the therapists joined Billy in enjoyable age-appropriate play. Finally, Billy and his father were encouraged to discover activities that they could enjoy together.

Hospitalization represented the desparate efforts of Mr. and Mrs. M. to pull themselves together so that the family could stay together. The treatment team enlarged on the family's resources, by using first themselves, then the family's friends, and finally the police. When his symptomatic behavior began to diminish, Billy was invited to replace it with play at a level of competence appropriate for his age and further encouraged to relate to his parents through mutually enjoyable activities.

Robbie R. was a 10-year-old diabetic boy who had been in and out of medical facilities for several years because of severe episodes of ketoacidosis. He always improved in the hospital, but relapsed shortly after returning home and getting back to school. Mr. and Mrs. R. had not been involved in Robbie's medical management, and his doctors had not been able to teach Robbie to care for himself. The lives of his parents totally revolved around Robbie and his diabetes. They were afraid to leave him alone, and they had cut themselves off from almost everyone, including their extended families, who were critical of their parenting and fearful of getting too close to Robbie because of his precarious health.

The R. family's admission to the hospital was conditional; in order to be admitted, the parents were required to take full responsibility for the management of Robbie's diabetes. The nursing staff was available to teach the parents what they needed to know, however, and the staff monitored the parents' monitoring of Robbie's diet and blood sugar levels. The rest of the staff assisted Mr. and Mrs. R. in helping Robbie to express his needs and feelings more directly.

After 2 weeks, the parents were thoroughly competent managers of their son and his diabetes, but the team felt that they might not sustain these accomplishments unless they had a life of their own, a life that did not revolve around Robbie. Therefore, Robbie's parents were asked to bring in their own parents, to teach them how to manage Robbie's diabetes (e.g., how to test his blood sugar level and what to do in case of an emergency), and to leave them in charge of Robbie while they, Robbie's parents, went away for the weekend. When they felt that they could enjoy time together without Robbie, they were discharged.

In this case, the therapeutic team created a context that activated the parents' competence to control their son's diabetes, to collaborate with the medical team directly, and to reconnect with their own families as resources. The hospital admission itself disrupted the symptomatic cycle, mobilizing the parents to do something they had previously been unable to do. Once they were in a position to care for their son, rather than leaving his care to the medical team, they could direct him to take care of himself.

USING SYMPTOMS

Symptoms are hooks to engage a family in therapy and the most direct access for a

therapist to enter a family system, but the removal of the symptoms is not the therapeutic goal. At the outset, listening to the family's presentation of the problem and trying to understand the family's struggle to cope with it helps the therapist both to join the family and to understand the structure that contributes to and maintains the symptoms. This information about the family's organization around a symptom is more useful than information about the symptom itself.

By joining with the family in its perception of reality, the therapist can develop a frame of reference that not only is meaningful to both the therapist and the family, but also helps individuals to see themselves differently in relation to others. The therapeutic team comes to resemble a storyteller. The family enters therapy with a particular story; therapy enlarges on the family's story, creating new outcomes of familiar themes. Everyone participates in the story's unfolding, enlarging it and creating scenarios that lead the family to more successful experiences and to elaborate their own story further.

The T. family consists of Ms. T. and her three children: Jason, aged 7; Julia, aged 6; and Jerome, aged 3. Also living in the household were Mrs. T., Ms. T's mother; Mr. H., Ms. T.'s paramour; and Sharon, Ms. T.'s older sister. The family was referred because Jason had set three large fires in the past several months. The school had repeatedly recommended that Ms. T. seek therapy for Jason because of behavior problems in the past, and she had made several appointments at the local community mental health center; she had kept none of them, however.

The entire treatment team was present for the assessment, either in the session or behind the mirror. They were struck by (1) Jason's shyness and sadness, (2) Ms. T.'s weight of approximately 300 pounds, (3) Ms. T.'s concern and caring for her children, (4) Ms. T.'s distance from other family members, (5) Sharon's activity in directing the children and criticizing their mother, and (6) the concern of Mrs. T. and Mr. H. for the children's well-being and their apparent lack of concern for Ms. T.

First, the therapist joined the family in mutual concern over Jason's firesetting, both as a signal of his difficulties and as a threat to the family's safety. The therapist carefully defined his view of Jason, saying that Jason was not a bad child, but rather was a child who seemed to be in great need of more consistency from his mother. The therapist also described Jason as immature and unable to communicate his needs effectively so that his firesetting might be a signal. The family members were opposed to placing Jason in a facility for emotionally disturbed children, but they acknowledged their fear that he would burn the house down. The more the therapist suggested that it might be too difficult for them to handle Jason and they might be better off if professional child care workers took over for them, the more the mother insisted that she wanted to raise him herself.

When asked if he thought that Jason's firesetting was at all related to his mother's depression and obesity, Mr. H. observed that Ms. T. had been moody and inconsistent with the children. He added that he worried about her physical and mental health and that other family members appeared to disregard her and undermine her parenting. Jason said that he was afraid of being beaten with the belt and left out in the street if he did bad things. He also expressed concern that his mother might go crazy or run away.

Ms. T. listened attentively and confirmed that, although she had often considered suicide, she never followed through because of her children. The therapist observed that she seemed to be living as if she were dead, allowing others to take over her responsibilities and to ridicule her in front of her children. The treatment team suggested that Jason might be setting fires (1) to kill his mother because he was furious with her for her inconsistency with him and his siblings, (2) to protect his mother from the deep pain she was suffering, and (3) to recruit help for himself, his mother, and the whole family, which seemed to be in the process of self-destructing. The T. family listened to these interpretations of Jason's symptoms and nodded silently in agreement.

At first, the therapeutic team was concerned that Jason's behavior was too dangerous for the apartment and suggested that the family should not be admitted until Ms. T. and Mr. H. had monitored Jason on a 24-hour basis for at least 3 days to prevent him from playing with matches. Instead, it was arranged that Mrs. T. would look after the other children at home while Ms. T. and Mr. H. worked with Jason in the hospital. The staff supervised Ms. T. and Mr. H. as they, in turn, supervised Jason.

The child's firesetting had become the means of securing the family's commitment to treatment. Separating the mother and her paramour from the other adults in the family allowed the staff to form a strong relationship with them and to begin to establish a subsystem boundary around Ms. T. and Mr. H. as a parental unit.

After the initial 3 days, Ms. T. was encouraged to teach her own mother what she had learned about caring for Jason. At the same time, she specified the help that she wanted from her mother. Ms. T. and Mr. H. spent the next week developing age-differentiated expectations for each of the three children; they resolved to be consistent, to set firm limits for the children, and to recognize accomplishments with compliments and hugs.

Ms. T. and Mr. H. quickly learned to manage the children more effectively. The therapist then expressed concern that there would be a relapse in Jason's behavior if his mother did not take better care of herself. Furthermore, Ms. T. would need to be on better terms with her extended family if she hoped to maintain her effectiveness with the children, because they would soon start testing her authority and probably would invite her mother and sister to criticize her once again.

Thus, the potential harm that she would be doing to her children if she remained obese and depressed motivated Ms. T. to change.

Ms. T. became very upset and revealed her longstanding rage at her sister, Sharon. When Ms. T. was between 10 and 14 years old, Sharon had sent her to prostitute herself so that Sharon could buy drugs. Ms. T. had never told her mother, who worked at night, because she thought it might cause her mother to have a heart attack. Sharon apparently had continued to use Ms. T. in different ways, verbally abusing her and criticizing her. Ms. T. felt that this relationship was a significant source of her depression, and she decided to work on resolving the matter.

With help from the therapeutic team, Ms. T. talked with her mother and obtained her support for a confrontation with Sharon. She then explained the situation to Mr. H., who also agreed to support her. They all agreed that Ms. T. would not be able to sustain her new high level of parenting if Sharon remained in the household, so Ms. T. and her mother were encouraged to expel Sharon from the house, giving her a specific date by which she had to be gone. Ms. T. wrote her sister a letter to express her outrage at the treatment she had received. Mrs. T.'s job was simply to confirm that Sharon must leave. In a letter to her oldest brother, Ms. T. expressed her understanding of the situation:

Came to find out, Jason's firesetting is because of me. I was fighting all the time to control my house, but I was not winning the fights and when I would lose fights, I would give up and stop fighting and start running away from them and my running away made the kids fight for themselves and they didn't know how to fight so Jason started setting fires. Jason almost killed himself because he was fighting with Sharon because I gave up and let her do what she wanted to do because everytime I tried to put her out she would call Mom and get her all worked up about it and I didn't want to make Mom sick so I had to put up with Sharon's shit. Then she got so that when I was in bed she'd be downstairs fucking with my kids. That's when she took Jason's last nerve and he set that last fire.

Jason's firesetting was the catalyst that caused his mother to cultivate support within her own family.

A final task focused on Ms. T.'s relationship with her paramour. Ms. T. told the staff about Mr. H.'s drinking and his violence toward her when he was on a spree. The team's one last fear was that, despite Mr. H.'s genuine love for the children, his lack of commitment would undo all the good work that had been done. The team felt that his commitment to Ms. T. could be a key to her well-being and her parental effectiveness. The therapist told Mr. H. that the solidarity of the family was at risk if he did not find a way to control his drinking, because he needed to have the energy and stability to be accessible and supportive to Ms. T.

In this family, Jason's symptom was used both as an explanation for family dysfunction and as an inducement to change.

FOCUSING ON PARENTS AS PARENTS

When a family with a severely symptomatic youngster seeks therapy, the straightforward approach is to help the parents cope with their child more effectively. It is assumed that, when the mother and father are more effective as parents, they will also be more comfortable in their other relationships, such as those with each other and with extended family members. It is best to postpone work on marital issues until the child's troublesome behavior is under control. In the end, marital therapy is often unnecessary, because working together as parents tends to bring the parents together as a couple.

In these critical situations that bring whole families into the hospital, members of the therapeutic team assume the role of parents to the parents, helping them to parent their children more effectively and to develop resourceful relationships with their own families and significant others. The position of the therapeutic team as nurturers of the parents allows the team both to model parenting and to empower the parents to discover ways to be effective with their children, thus placing the expertise on these particular children within the family.

In each of the cases described, the therapeutic team played such a parental role. In the M. family, for example, the team did not control the child, but supervised while the parents mustered their own resources (e.g., friends and police).

In the R. family, the team encouraged the parents to replace the medical experts in their child's life. Finally, in the T. family, the team actively parented Ms. T., guiding her in small steps with many challenges and a great deal of support. Team members observed her interactions with her children, made suggestions, and gave her support and positive reinforcement with each successful move. For example, they worked with Ms. T. and Jason on his homework, modeling clear expectations and patience by being clear and patient with Ms. T. as she was working with Jason. They complimented her when she did well, and she would do the same with Jason. This routine was practiced day after day.

In the overall treatment plan the team functioned as parent to Ms. T. Their expectations of the family were made extremely clear: first, that the parents would need to come into the inpatient unit to supervise Jason closely for the three days; second, that the mother was not allowed to threaten abandonment of the children or of treatment; third, that discharge was contingent on clarifying things with Sharon and getting her to leave the house; and fourth, that discharge was also contingent on a more effective system of conflict resolution between Ms. T. and Mr. H. The family was kept secure in the apartment context until the new structures were solid enough to withstand the stresses of life outside the hospital without the consistent presence of the treatment team. Like an old-fashioned father-in-law, the therapist was very direct with Mr. H. during the discharge phase. He told him simply what he had to do to work on his relationship with Ms. T. There was no argument; Mr. H. was grateful for the therapist's honesty.

The position of the treatment team in relation to the children becomes something like that of grandparents, but the team sidesteps some of the natural hazards of three-generational systems. One of the staff members may block a child's attempt to obtain the staff member's support against the parent, for example, sending the message that the parents are in charge. In this way, the team also models an effective relationship with grandparents. On the other hand, the team may create a situation in which one therapist or a staff member deliberately crosses generational boundaries and supports the child against the parents, as an intrusive grandparent might do, while another staff member helps the parents to confront this undermining of their authority and to make it clear that they are in charge of decisions regarding the child.

A parent's competence may be further supported and strengths used by putting the parent in a position of authority over a group that includes the parent's own child and his or her peers. Asking a mother to oversee a classroom project based on an area of her expertise is one way to do this.

In the context of the apartments, parents find a firm, consistent, clear set of directives that support their own effectiveness with their children, underscore their competence, and encourage their creativity on a 24-hour basis every day.

ENHANCING PLAYFULNESS

Most families in which there are serious disturbances find themselves besieged both by their children's misbehavior and by the blame that others level at them because of the children's problems. Under these circumstances, playing may be the last thing that occurs to them. Young children invite play, however, and it is an important medium through which parents can connect with their children (Keith & Whitaker, 1981).

Play was a major feature of treatment for the P. family, which consisted of Mrs. P., aged 24 and divorced, and her 8-year-old son, Maurice. Mrs. P. also has a daughter; she was living with Mrs. P.'s parents, however, because Mrs. P. was having so many problems with Maurice.

Maurice and his mother had frequent contacts with child protective services. Maurice had been abused, and he was aggressive, fearful, and mistrustful. He had a history of hoarding food and stealing from stores; most recently, he had been setting fires. His mother's difficulty in controlling him easily became anger and physical abuse. She recognized this problem and feared that she would hurt him badly and be sent to jail. Mrs. P. admitted to feeling depressed and choked by her responsibilities. She was tired of having to deal with the police or the school authorities. Distant from her own family, she felt isolated and lonely. She showed Maurice little affection.

Admission of the P. family to the apartment was contingent on a promise from Mrs. P. never to threaten Maurice with abandonment. Recognizing how entrenched mother and child were in the attacking and

inciting attack cycle, the therapeutic team members committed themselves to assist Mrs. P. in a step-by-step process to reshape her relationship with Maurice. They took on various roles with Mrs. P., including those of peers, parents, and co-parent. In essence, the team created for the P. family a community that, unlike their beleaguered and isolated existence outside the hospital, was rich in responsiveness and companionship. In this context, two therapeutic interventions were particularly significant.

The first occurred during the therapist's daily meetings with the family, often over breakfast, when the therapist would chat with both mother and son. When the therapist saw Mrs. P. begin to react to Maurice in a harsh, attacking manner, he would say something like "I really don't appreciate your paying more attention to your provocative son than to me when I am trying to talk with you. You seem to find him more interesting than you find me. Please let me know if you want me to leave, or if you find me boring. If not, I would appreciate it if you would show me more respect by not being so easily pulled to him when we are talking, especially when he is acting in some immature, obnoxious way, as 8-year-olds do." Mrs. P. generally softened and laughed at these kinds of comments. She and the therapist would laugh together, and she would generally return to the conversation with the therapist. With each of Maurice's interruptions, his mother set a boundary between herself and her son more quickly and matter-of-factly.

The second intervention that was especially effective involved the therapist's attention to Maurice. The therapist began to play with the boy, focusing on the constructive, age-appropriate aspects of his behavior and dismissing the provocative aspects. They embarked on several projects together, following Maurice's interests. As Mrs. P. appeared to relax and enjoy her son's interaction with the therapist, she was invited to join with them. These experiences began in therapy sessions; were reinforced by Mrs. P.'s observations and presence with her son in the therapeutic classroom; and continued on field trips to the park, the zoo, and the Please Touch Museum. It was quickly discovered that Maurice behaved very well when he was exposed to a diversity of experiences with his mother and the focus was not on his misbehavior. As the staff played with the animals at the zoo, made funny faces and noises in response to the monkeys, and touched the different objects and toys at the museum, Mrs. P. began to be more playful. At first shocked by his mother's behavior, Maurice began to follow suit, assuming a more trusting childlike posture with his mother.

With these different perceptions of herself and her son, as well as staff support, Mrs. P. was able to work with the school authorities to find an appropriate setting for Maurice, and she helped to get him settled in his new school before their discharge from the apartment. Outpatient therapy continued to help in the management of Maurice's occasional school crises and, when these abated, to work with the mother on her personal problems. Mrs. P. stopped therapy when she became seriously involved with a man and was attending school full-time.

Clearly, Mrs. P. was in no mood to play when first referred, nor did Maurice exhibit age-appropriate playfulness. To the contrary, Maurice seemed far too preoccupied with behaviors that indicated his desparate clinging to his relationship with his mother. Their entire relationship was restructured on the basis of the playfulness that developed between the staff and the mother and between the mother and the child.

REFERENCES

Anderson, C. (1977). Family intervention with severely disturbed inpatients. *Archives of General Psychiatry, 34*, 697–702.

Bowen, M. (1966). Family psychotherapy with schizophrenia in the hospital and private practice. In I. Boszormenyi-Nagy & J.L. Framo (Eds.), *Intensive family therapy* (pp. 117–146). New York: Harper & Row.

Brendler, J. (1983). Brief hospitalization of whole families. Kalmon Flomenhaft (Chair), *New frontiers in family therapy*. Presented at symposium conducted at Downstate Medical Center, Brooklyn, New York.

Castaneda, C. (1972). *Journey to Ixtlan*, New York: Simon and Schuster.

Combrinck-Graham, L. (1985). Hospitalization as a therapeutic intervention in the family. In R. Ziffer (Ed.), *Adjunctive techniques in family therapy* (pp. 99–124). Orlando, FL: Grune & Stratton.

Combrinck-Graham, L., Gursky, E.J., & Brendler, J. (1982). Hospitalization of single-parent families of disturbed children. *Family Process, 21*, 141–152.

Grunebaum, H.U., & Weiss, J.L. (1963). Psychotic mothers and their children in joint admission to an adult psychiatric hospital. *American Journal of Psychiatry, 119*, 927–933.

Keith, D.V., & Whitaker, C.A. (1981). Play ther-apy: A paradigm for work with families. *Journal of Marital and Family Therapy, 7*, 243–254.

Langsley, D.G., & Kaplan, D.M. (1968). *Treatment of families in crisis.* New York: Grune & Stratton.

Nakhla, F., Folkart, L., & Webster, J. (1969). Treatment of families as in-patients. *Family Process, 8*, 79–95.

Index